TOOLS FOR THE PRESCHOOL YEARS

TOOLS FOR THE PRESCHOOL YEARS

Support for time-crunched, mobile, multitasking parents of 3-6 year olds

Yvonne Gustafson, PhD

Illustrated by Greg Bonnell

To my Clan—biological and chosen—
thank you for sharing who you are with me.

—Yvonne

Learn more at www.your-parenting-matters.com

For parents of younger children, see Yvonne's first book:
*Tools for the Toddler Years: Parenting support for the time-crunched, always
interrupted, mobile, multi-tasking parents of toddlers*

Copyright © 2018 by Yvonne Gustafson, PhD
Illustrated by Greg Bonnell

Book Design & Production: Columbus Publishing Lab
www.ColumbusPublishingLab.com

LCCN: 2018959452
Paperback ISBN: 978-1-63337-226-9
E-book ISBN: 978-1-63337-227-6

Printed in the United States of America
1 3 5 7 9 10 8 6 4 2

CONTENTS

INTRODUCTION

Did you pick up this book for a preview of life with a preschooler? Perhaps, you are looking for a solution for a specific problem? It's possible you may have picked it up for some reassurance in the face of all the social noise about children and parents. If you read the earlier book, *Tools for the Toddler Years*, you know to expect this book to have a variety of content across several child and family domains, some of which may feel like enrichment—good to know but not particularly necessary or helpful in the moment. However, much of the content of this book is directed at the key elements of child development and adult leadership strategies that will support parents and caregivers dealing with the day-to-day challenges of guiding preschool children. It is hoped that by offering enrichment and problem-solving content, there will also be reassurance that whatever the challenge it can be resolved with more reliable information.

This book is designed with brief sections to support you—the parent with little time to read:

- Information in this book is designed to connect developmental whys and hows with guidance strategies that are attentive to parental stressors, adult and child needs, and overall family dynamics.

- The content in this book reflects those issues that most often perplex, challenge, and exhaust parents.

- You will find support for day-to-day challenges, so that day-to-day you can experience the joy of parenting and feel capable, loving, and confident in your leadership. As a result, in turn, you are better able to nurture a capable, loving, and confident child.

HOW TO READ ANY PARENTING BOOK

Listen to the expert—you

There is no secret, no special trick. As inviting as a parenting formula may be, always be skeptical of one-stop solutions. Parenting is an art, practiced by you, supported by others—family, friends, teachers, and we hope, this parenting book. So, if you're looking for an expert on your child, you've already found it—you.

Because of your hands-on care, you will know best if your child responds to singing ("Let's get in the car so we can sing along with your CD"), or if she loves ritual, silliness, or the very concrete message of a chart or timer. Parental intuition is not to be ignored. (But, if you feel yours has been disrupted by a difficult childhood or trauma, it helps to have a trusted individual who can listen long enough for you to find clarity.)

Get to know the expert

Along with understanding your child, understanding yourself is an important element of parenting. It will also help you to make the best use of the strategies and knowledge offered in a parenting book. For instance, a person who tends toward a more indulgent parenting style might understand the parenting tool "acknowledgment of hard work" quite differently from someone more familiar with a rigid style. One parental lens takes it as a possible endorsement of bribery. Another sees coddling. Understanding that the personal lens exists makes it possible to see the tool for what it is—a simple reminder about cause and effect and motivation, all key to human activity at any age.

Make it a conversation

Many of us tend to think of books as definitive sources. We suggest that you think of the parenting book more like you would a friend. You rely on your friends for ideas, support, understanding, and the best knowledge they can share, but you do not expect your friends to have all the answers or for their answers to be right for you all the time. The parenting book is one voice, a valued and knowledgeable voice (or it should be), but still one voice in a bigger conversation.

Choose your friends wisely

"Consider the source" is an especially useful adage as you decide what written support is best for you and your family. Because parenting is such a complex task, many respected fields of study contribute to the pool of information and advice. Physicians bring a focus on health; psychologists bring an emphasis on relationship building; neuroscientists and child developmental researchers bring attention to change, growth, and milestones. It is not only faith-based authors who frame parenting within a set of beliefs. Every author brings personal and professional values to his or her work.

Do a gut check

Always test advice against your own intuition and values. Take for example two kinds of advice you may have been given about infant sleep. Crying to sleep is an effective sleep strategy vs. meet your baby's needs so he doesn't cry. Sometimes when using the cry-it-out strategy, Mom is crying harder than baby. For this mom, the cry-it-out strategy is probably not a good fit for the family right now. It may be that at an intuitive level she is reading a different need for her child, or that she does not yet fully believe her child is ready for this developmental demand.

When the strategy does not fit the parent's values, it is much harder to follow-through, and it is, therefore, much less likely to work. But, even if it did work, it would do little to support the parental self-confidence that will be needed to face the next parenting challenge.

APPROACH AND PHILOSOPHY

This book is centered in the understanding that parenting with respect, affection, and support makes kids feel confident and loved, and makes parents feel successful and loving. This is not a trademark philosophy, nor is it aligned with any other. This approach is based on the understanding that, no matter the latest craze, parenting is always about warmth and control. The advice, tools, and strategies offered here seek a balance of these two so that the child feels nurtured, secure, and loved (warmth), as well as valued and listened to, while given clear boundaries and appropriate expectations (control).

This approach is shared by many. It is supported by research in psychology, neuroscience, and parent education. It is reflected in the lived-wisdom of many from past generations. It has also been illustrated, charted, and graphed—many times over. You'll find a version of this on page 57, where four quadrants illustrate four different ways of balancing warmth and control. Below is the quadrant that best demonstrates the balance we seek to offer parents.

AUTHORITATIVE/DEMOCRATIC

POSSIBLE BELIEF SYSTEM:

Everyone in this family counts. My job is to love, coach and guide.

WHAT IT CAN LOOK LIKE AT THIS AGE:

- Free cuddles and smiles
- Recognizable rhythm to the day
- Acknowledgment rather than praise
- Clear, direct teaching about rules
- Consistent reminders with natural and logical consequences for child's behavior choices

PARENTS CAN BE:

- Firm, but not rigid
- Respectful
- Cooperative
- Freely affectionate
- Aware of adult and child needs/wants

Everything in this book is also based in the following beliefs:

- Parenting is an art, practiced by you, and supported by the wisdom and research of others. There is no one-size-fits-all solution that will benefit every parent-child-family context.

- Parenting is joyful serious stuff. It's an important job, as we often hear, but rarely is it acknowledged as an interesting and engaging job. Nurturing children is inherently impactful; it is wonderfully complex, fascinating, and can be fun.

- Children are human beings. Not drama queens. Not whiners. Not a label at all. (See *Labels Impact Life*, page 131.)

- Parents are smart and capable people who look for and deserve support they can trust. The mission stemming from this belief becomes an effort to provide parents with solid information, concrete strategies, clear examples from actual families, insight into child development, and encouragement to frame problems in a positive way. When claiming a positive frame, the mind is open to build unique solutions that work for self, family, and the special, fully-faceted, complex human beings children are.

- No book will answer every question, nor be perfect. Errors do occur. When faced with a potential error the adult will seek further clarity.

LANGUAGE AND OTHER PRACTICALITIES

Most often this is written about children in the plural to avoid categorizing any behavior as strictly male or female. However, when not possible, in these pages the preschool child is sometimes a he, sometimes a she. The pronouns are used randomly, to honor the gifts of gender.

Likewise, parents are sometimes Mom, sometimes Dad.

There is nothing in this book that can be used to justify any kind or type of harmful, abusive, disrespectful, neglectful, or dangerously indulgent acts.

This book is made for the specific needs of the parent or caregiver of preschool children. Some reference will be made to early elementary children (K plus or K+) to support those who have children straddling the next developmental stage. At the close of this book we hope it will have provided you with tools and strategies, as well as a deeper understanding of the development of your preschooler. And further, that you feel the respect and support for the physical, emotional, and spiritual stamina it takes to do the best you can for your child, your family, and yourself.

PART I:
THE CHILD

THE HARDWORKING CHILD

Parents have come to expect that meeting milestones for walking and talking and birth-to-three brain development are important—and they are! When we place so much focus on what happens in the earliest years, we forget to cue parents that brain development and physical and social development continue, and in ways just as fascinating and celebratory.

The physical growth spurts that trigger new shoes and longer shirts are obvious. Conflicts with siblings and peers, struggles with fears, and new behavioral choices are cues, though far less obvious, to mental and emotional growth spurts. These spurts, which might bring a new fear of the dark or resistance to parental leadership, can leave many parents confused—some even wondering where their sweet child has gone, and who exactly has taken his or her place!

Although each broad domain of development—physical, emotional, mental—is meshed with the others, they can also be out of sync with one another. Literally, children can sound like short adults while at the same time be very young in the way they manage their bodies and their emotions. The opposite of looks being deceiving, a child's verbal maturity can lead us to expect, unfairly, that the child should behave in an equally mature way.

PHYSICAL

From infancy through toddlerhood, the body changes in amazing ways. Though more subtle in older children, the amazing changes keep coming. The preschool child, roughly three to six years old, has begun to integrate large muscles. No longer physically awkward, she steps freely from stairs to floor or may even jump the last step and land fully balanced on both feet. It no longer troubles her to change walking surfaces from grass to sidewalk to the mulch under the playground equipment. She can easily shift from walking to running, and climbing is a celebration often shared by a bright call of, "See me! I'm queen of the fort!" as her physical skills become an asset in her imaginative play world. With all this big muscle development, everything about play is likely to be larger, louder, and more intense than it was just a few months before.

With all this new skill and energy, it may seem like a great time to introduce children to team sports. There are, however, developmental considerations that may shape children's ultimate experience. First, preschool children are just beginning to understand the nature of play that requires staying within a narrow set of rules, making it hard for them to enjoy activities that are defined by rules. And, since foot and eye coordination may not fully develop until age nine or ten, children may feel pressured to perform beyond their body's development. Which means that even the most physically adept preschool child will be challenged by organized sports except at the most basic level.

At three years, boys are roughly 53% of their adult height. For little girls it is closer to 57%. You may want to check their baby book or measure them now and make your guess.

GROSS DOES NOT MEAN *YUCKY!*

Gross motor development refers to the large muscles of the body—the arms and legs. Fine motor refers to the small muscles—the hands and fingers that involve more control of small objects like the tools for writing. The small muscles of the hands and fingers are often weaker than they appear. Early on, it is far easier to take off a garment than to put it on. Buttons and zippers are a challenge. It is easier to stack a large block than to manage to keep a color inside a line. (Who needs to anyway?) Large-grasp tools will be needed until fingers are stronger and more coordinated or hands might cramp and pain may be associated with the learning environment.

Every parent would agree that there is nothing inherently wrong with running—on the playground, but not at the grocery store. Likewise, there's nothing wrong with using strong muscles to climb—but please not the cupboards. It's hard not to be charmed by those squeals of delight over the game of tag in the backyard—but at the library, it's a different story. So along with this body work, there is also the social demand to learn when and where to be faster, stronger, and louder.

It's not a bad thing for children to be fast, strong, or loud. The challenge for them, and for the adults in their lives, is to figure out **when** and **where** these traits are best expressed.

Another challenge is *how much*. It is not always easy to regulate *how fast*, *how much muscle to use*, and *how much volume* to generate, and for many young bodies it is *all or nothing*. Your reminder to your preschooler to "walk" lasted what, three steps? That hug for baby brother turned into an infant in distress, sibling roughhousing resulted in tears, and those happy, sharp squeals may be enough for anyone to want to run and hide for relief.

> Play materials like Play-Doh or snap-together building blocks do the work of strengthening fingers while disguised as playful fun.

A further challenge for children and parents is the lack of body awareness related to space. As a young child, if I climb on the slide's ladder, I will not be aware that I am too close to the child before me and may be bumped or stepped on as they climb. If I'm in a ball pit with another child, my friend will not know to allow space for me if he chooses to sprawl in the balls. If I'm running, I will not be able to be attentive to the movement of others to avoid crashes.

Added to all of those limitations, very few children can predict harm to themselves or others. As a preschool child, I am unlikely to recognize that my too-tight hug could do injury to a pet. I cannot easily predict that my steps away from my swing will put me in the path of the other. I may not know that crashing my riding toy into my friend's riding toy could either damage the toy or hurt the other rider. As a preschooler, I won't recognize that my boots could hurt Mom as she's strapping me in my car seat. Even in early elementary, I may be moving too fast to stop myself from causing harm.

All of this adds up to the need for adults to be aware as children play. Some believe an emphasis on safe, durable toys and play equipment are a must as they do this important developmental work. Others believe that exploration and body awareness are best developed in a less controlled environment. Whatever the choice of play environments provided, ultimately it is the responsibility of the adults in children's lives to function as insurance against significant injury.

For the child, these new skills sure are fun, but they can also get me in trouble! I can sometimes lift a gallon of milk but I can't pour it! I can use my scooter and maybe even a bike, but I can't predict that I could be hurt if I go beyond the driveway. I can love to tumble with my friend and still not know how to be safe next to him as we wiggle. That wiggle and giggle can quickly become tears with no intent to hurt.

I can also get in trouble by using my body to problem-solve. Grabbing a toy from a younger sibling or friend is efficient, but now I find that my friends are quick to take it back or the adults insist that I figure out how to "use my words." This body is great, and it takes a lot of work to learn all the social rules that are required to manage it.

And those words…Although by age three I have over 1,000, my speech may still have some articulation issues. The tongue is a muscle too, and takes a while to become coordinated and for all the sounds of speech to be integrated and controlled. (See *A Guide to Normal Speech Development*, page 21.)

The inability to manage multiple layers of awareness frightens every driver who passes children playing in a yard with a ball. A child focused on the ball will not be able to shift focus to approaching traffic. New virtual reality computer games may have children moving around as they play, creating another context in which they are not aware of risks.

MORE GROWTH...BODY/MIND/SPIRIT

Body regulation supports social skills. In addition to learning to cope with the demands of imagination and accompanying fears, children enter the world of independent peer play. This independence from the immediate presence of the adult means that children must learn to become collaborative players, use speech to expand play, negotiate turns with peers, figure out the rules of social interaction, and learn to play in ways that are safe and enjoyable. This huge personal assignment means being able to manage impulse control. (See the *Shadowing* section, page 46.)

Impulse control is not something that we learn once in life, like riding a bike. **Impulse control requires the engagement of the mind, body, and spirit.** Using an example from adult life: limiting dessert. The mind can list all the reasons to limit desserts, the body can move away from the dessert table at a buffet, and the spirit can judge or celebrate the results that will either discourage or reinforce further attempts to limit desserts. For children three and older, the mind, the body, and the spirit are all beginning to acquire the skills that underlie impulse control.

The **mind**, for instance, is learning the social rules for playing with others. This means moving to the more sophisticated and abstract tool of speech rather than the grab and go of a toddler. It means planning for turns. As preschool children begin to develop the skills of elementary children, they will become interested in learning specific rules of board games and sports to define the nature of the play. They begin to incorporate a functional understanding of values, using broad labels of good and bad.

The **body** is learning to match the intensity of movement to the environment. We use our

The child's brain is driven to explore and solve any and all puzzles. This is why we encourage parents to consider those "safety caps" not as childproof, but as a child delay feature that will allow the adult extra moments to get to the child and secure anything that could cause harm. This is significant in other contexts where older children may find humor in leading smaller children into trouble.

inside voices when indoors. We run on playgrounds, not in stores. We learn to stop before injuring others or ourselves through recognizing our own inner sense of slow, medium, fast, and stop. When parents say "slow down!" they are directing children to pay attention to their bodies, recognize the speed, and direct attention to the muscles to set another pace.

The **spirit** reinforces impulse control skills through claiming personal satisfaction in being able to manage oneself, enjoy companionship, and build satisfying friendships.

SPEECH, WORDS...*STORY*

With speech comes words, and almost immediately after: story. For children, these are the stories Mom and Dad read to me, the stories of our day together, the stories that help me understand how things work. In fact, this process is so important that it seems hardwired into parents to encourage children to tell stories and to use them to practice not only the art of telling, but also the benefit of oral rehearsal (repeating rules or routines as reminders).

"How did Thomas the Train help his friend when he was sad?"

"Tell Grandma about the lion we saw at the zoo…"

"What's our rule about jumping on the sofa?" (Remember they need to practice telling the story many times before they can use story to guide their own behavior.)

It is often through questions used to expand on stories that children categorize a great amount of content. Not only facts—sky is blue and it is up—but also social context—dishes go with the kitchen area of the classroom. Kindergarten+ children may begin to expand their moral decision-making through stories of heroes both real and imaginary.

Teachers expand on the process of questioning to help children become aware of the context in which characters are involved in the story, or to expand children's enjoyment of the reading experience.

In highly literate cultures, children soon learn books can both give information and provide entertainment. Children who are also readers are still likely to enjoy having an adult read to them. This may become a special time for connection before bed or for quiet time in the afternoon. For younger children, sometimes, long before they

Asking "did you," or "why did you," invites the developing mind to seek story to give an answer. As children generate a story they may be accused of being a liar. Although the story may be an untruth as the adult sees it, there is a difference between the primary lying of a preschool child and lying done by an elementary age child. (For more information on primary lying **see *Why the Lies*, page 95.**)

can actually decipher letters and words, they will "read to themselves" by turning the pages and telling the story as they remember the words from the big people in their lives.

From a brain growth view, the development of speech is often accompanied by a major shift in play. Children actively enter play that expresses a story. For younger children, tucking in a baby doll for sleep has a corresponding story that has a beginning, middle, and end. Parents may hear the words of the family bedtime ritual or abbreviated songs that have become the "way it happens in our house." Little ones may invite parents to pretend meals in which they are the providers. Or when parents are serving as a child's playmate they may be directed to drive a toy car to a particular location or down a particular path. On one level, children are modeling and rehearsing the patterns of life in their families and further integrating them into the scaffolding of their brain structure. At another level, they are practicing being in charge of themselves (claiming self-efficacy) and expanding their understanding of how the world works.

The transition to board games and other rule-driven play evolves from this early social play. Children will struggle to adjust to a form of play in which turn-taking is a requirement and in which there are winners and losers rather than collaborative playmates. It may take several months before children can manage the disappointment associated with this form of play.

This need for being in charge of oneself is seen in other day-to-day interactions, from expressions such as, "do it myself," and resistance across several domains—napping, teeth brushing, etc. This can be especially frustrating for parents who have been in charge of when, where, and how things happen in the family.

SPEECH, WORDS, STORY... *IMAGINATION*

Further, the gift of story associated with this brain growth spurt is also the entry into an inner life with imagination. Although we can love the creativity associated with imagination, we don't love that our children can now literally scare themselves with their own imaginative stories. "Monsters" may enter the picture, and normal sounds of the house may now spark fear. The toddler who would sleep through a thunderstorm is now a preschooler panicked by the rumbling noises. Before, a dead bird would have been seen, but not necessarily illicit the need for additional comforting or understanding. For a preschooler, however, a dead bird may cause parents to deal with huge questions of what it means to be dead, or why a bird has died.

These are huge questions from people who often sound like short adults but do not process information in the same context as an adult. This represents a challenge for parents who must work with both intelligence (smart) and maturity (age/development). In life, they are meshed as we balance our inner lives and external demands for problem-solving, but for the purposes of understanding, it can sometimes be helpful to pull them apart. A child can have an intellect that supports a huge vocabulary and conversation skills, yet still have a limited ability to understand because of brain development. Fantasy and reality are meshed, making it almost impossible for the child to sort out the "reality" of the imagined monster and the "reality" of Dad standing before them. After all, the child sees both of them.

> The emotion centers of the brain are directly behind the ears. Surprising and loud sounds can easily trigger emotional responses in children (of all ages). Until children are old enough to recognize which sounds may signal danger, they may react strongly and need support.

FEELINGS AND COPING STRATEGIES

This stage of development demands that children begin to learn to cope with

Until about middle elementary, children think in very concrete terms. A skilled Child Life Specialist reminded her colleagues that common phrases can be especially frightening in healthcare settings. "They're just going to take your blood"; "they will put you to sleep for your surgery" (especially frightening if they've had a pet who's been "put to sleep"); "they're going to take you on a stretcher." Being aware of the literal way in which these phrases may be interpreted will be helpful in discussing BIG topics with concrete thinkers.

feelings—those generated by imagination, and those of frustration and disappointment when they cannot be in charge of themselves or a situation. It may seem at times that children's emotional responses are "out of proportion" to the events that trigger them. Without an understanding of the challenges children face in learning emotional and physical self-regulation it may be tempting to label children "drama queens" or "too sensitive" when adults do not perceive the event as the child does. Well-intended reassurance that "it is not a big deal" denies the reality that for the child it FEELS like a very big deal. Although coping strategies will expand and mature over time, children often begin to express patterns of preferred coping.

Let's take a moment to expand on some common behaviors (or seeds of coping patterns) we may see in children who are learning to cope, and how they might be expressed later as an adult.

"Learn About"

Preschool years are prime time for a dinosaur obsession. From a logical point of view, there is no reason why a child would focus so fully on ancient animals. They do not see them at the zoo. There are no large dinosaur bones lying about the backyard to pique their interest. However, the brain growth spurt has cued the child to a much larger world, and although being a "big kid" sounds good, it is also scary. This brain growth means that some children will experience a generalized anxiety, and since they also have a mind that must problem-solve through concrete means, they will need ways to express their developing capacity to manage fear. For these children, the "learn about" strategy is a particularly useful tool. "Learn about" may take the form of, "If I know everything there is to know about dinosaurs, then I can better manage my fears." So, I may learn how to identify *and pronounce* each dinosaur name, separate the plant eaters and the hunters, and how many millions of years ago they died (even as I have a fairly underdeveloped sense of time). Dinosaurs are big and powerful, but they are also gone. Huge and dead are both pretty serious concepts I'm managing through my efforts to "learn about."

A variation of this pattern can be seen in children who benefit from oral rehearsal—a form of pre-telling and pre-planning to minimize the power of surprise. Please note the importance of knowing the child in your life. It is possible that for particular children, too many reminders of something that is coming will actually increase anxiety, rather than help them to manage it.

In adulthood, this coping strategy may be seen in adults who do detail planning in preparation for change, or who search the web for the minutia of treatment details in the face of an illness. They will "take charge" of anxiety by "learning about" it.

"Come Be by Me"

Some children will resist going to bed on their own. These are children who use a coping strategy lightly referred to as "come be by me." For example, having managed the transition to independent sleep as a toddler, now as an older child I *need* Mom or Dad to stay with me until I sleep. (**For bedtime issues see** *Sleep*, **page 169.**)

In adulthood, this coping strategy can lead people to maintain a close community of support. Taking a friend along to share things that feel new or different will continue to be a buffer for stress.

"Call in the Troops"

Some children under stress will cry, whine, or begin to "act out." These behaviors are literally strategies that "call in the troops for help." Since parents can rarely ignore these behaviors, displaying distress in this manner can guarantee attention even if that attention is negative. Brief periods of regression—behavior usually associated with a prior developmental stage—are often seen at the transition to having a new baby in the house, or some other milestone such as entry into all-day school.

Although this strategy may "work" for the very young, in adults it can alienate family and friends or create a family context in which members "walk on eggshells" to avoid triggering stress in the other.

The preschool years are a time in which children can begin to be taught not only to pay attention to their body's signs of stress, but also to use calming strategies to help them access the resources for self-regulation when in stressful environments. (For an example, see *How the Remote Can Teach Your Child Self-Control*, page 38.)

Overwhelm

Another pattern seen in children under stress is rigid body resistance. This is when the body is overwhelmed by stress hormones to the point of "freeze, flight, or fight." At this point of overwhelm, children cannot be calmed through reason. It may take extensive time for a child to physically calm enough to enter into problem-solving or explore alternate coping strategies. One variation of "flight" is the attempt to take oneself out of the picture, either physically or mentally. But keep in mind that preschool children live in the moment, and they may actually have "moved on" in a way that an elementary child fleeing to a video game may not have.

As an adult, avoiding new places or hesitating to take advantage of new opportunities may reflect a pattern from early childhood of physical freezing or fleeing stress. A phrase like, "I was so scared I couldn't think," may be a sign of an adult who has experienced a flood of stress hormone.

Helper Coping

A further example of a seed of coping can be seen in children who take steps to manage their external world by becoming a "helper" for parents or siblings. It can be a wonderful gift to have a sibling who helps with difficult shoes or carries groceries into the house. However, taking on tasks with the intent to keep siblings or Mom happy, may be more about managing the emotional environment than practicing leadership or self-care skills.

At its most extreme, "helper coping" adults jump into care for others without acknowledging the boundaries of personal responsibility (doing for others what they should be doing for themselves). It can become a danger of emotional depletion if helping others is seen as more important than self-care. On the other hand, the positive expression of altruistic-helper coping is often a general sense of service and caring within a family or community. It is probably most significantly displayed by adults who, though experiencing their own significant loss, find ways to offer support for others experiencing the same or similar loss.

Every coping pattern has value. In maturity, strategies that enable people to go on without confronting the stress are generally thought to be useful for short-term issues or as an immediate response to crisis. For long-term challenges, strategies that both acknowledge and accept have been found to be more useful. As people grow, they are able to develop and use multiple coping strategies.

Coping strategies are just one way that children begin to express their developing sense of identity. Brain-emotional development has components shaped through relationships, as well as through the unique internal life of an independent human being. Parents will hear hints of developing self-identity in personal celebrations of, "I'm strong"; "I'm big"; "I'm a good big brother."

Why? Why? Why?:
Nurturing Their Curiosity and Your Sanity

If "The Whys" are driving you crazy, there is a good reason. We can passively listen or even tune in and out of a monologue, but questions, by nature, put us on alert. "Why?" piques us to respond. Thus, despite how much we adore our children's burgeoning curiosity, it is common for the continual "whys" to become irritating.

What to Do

"The Whys" are part of your child's verbal processing of the world. It is a good developmental sign, but if it is driving you crazy, here's how to get some relief without discouraging your child:

Redirect

"You tell me. What do you think?" By repeating back the answer you already gave, the child is also helping herself to anchor the information. Tap into the child's need to feel competent: "You've learned a lot already/you know a lot. Go tell baby brother/ the kitty/your stuffed animals what you think the answer is."

Use Music

Sing a song or make up a song. The song doesn't necessarily have to answer the litany of questions. The simple act of singing can offer an outlet for all the words in the child's head. Singing can allow the child to do the verbal processing she needs to do, but in a way that is less irritating to you.

A Guide to Normal Speech Development

Vowel sounds are produced correctly by 90% of all children by age three. However, consonant sounds may not come until much later.

The following provides a general guideline for the age at which 90% of children will consistently express these consonant sounds in their speech.

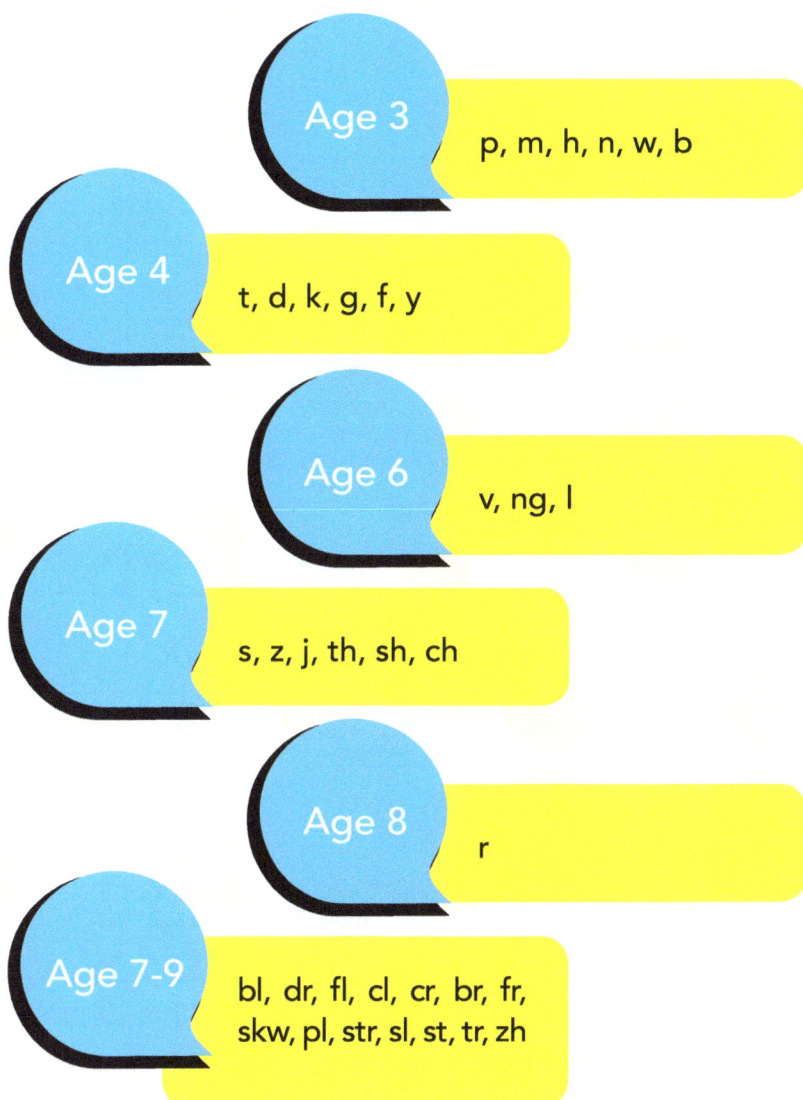

Age 3 — p, m, h, n, w, b

Age 4 — t, d, k, g, f, y

Age 6 — v, ng, l

Age 7 — s, z, j, th, sh, ch

Age 8 — r

Age 7-9 — bl, dr, fl, cl, cr, br, fr, skw, pl, str, sl, st, tr, zh

IS IT OK TO USE OK?

THE DIFFERENCE BETWEEN WHAT ADULTS MEAN AND WHAT CHILDREN HEAR

"Do they make pencils in Pennsylvania?"

Once you hear it, this question from the mouth of a child makes perfect sense. Yet it is a question almost no adult would think to ask.

The English language is multifaceted and complex, sometimes delightfully so, sometimes confusingly so. To make sense of it, we rely on contextual information and our understanding of the speaker's intentions. As adults, we do this so intuitively, unconsciously, and seamlessly that it would not occur to us to ask if pencils are indeed made in Pennsylvania.

But, as young children do the day-to-day hard work of matching meaning to language, not only do they have fewer life experiences to draw on, the way they experience the world is markedly different from that of an adult. To give just one example, because of the way the brain develops, the young toddler brain cannot understand past and future. But the adult brain cannot NOT understand past and future.

Another important difference: abstract vs. literal thought.

Try sometime to interpret a conversation literally. You'll find that it is hard (your language skills are just that good). But you'll also see how the words adults say—even as we think we are being perfectly clear—can be so easily misinterpreted.

Now, add words with multiple meanings into the mix and things can get even more complicated. For example, is *cool* describing temperature or demeanor? Is it an affirmation or positive judgment?

And then there's this word...the one that parents use all the time and one that can mean any number of things—*OK*.

"OK" is so multipurpose that it can be used to express enthusiasm *("OK! Let's go!")* AND disappointment *("I'm feeling OK, I guess...")*. It can be an expression of agreement (yes, it's OK), judgment (OK that's enough), or approval (OK by me).

While adults can easily sort out the intended meaning of an "OK," we cannot expect the same from a literal thinker who is still coming to understand the variables of context and intent. So, when Mom or Dad says, *"It's time to go to bed, OK?"*

...is the parent asking the child to agree with her proposal?

...making a judgment about the child's understanding of the time?

...asking the child to give her permission?

Most parents don't ask their child for permission to set a bedtime. Yet many parents will tag an "OK" onto the end of a non-negotiable statement. It's common to use "OK" in order to make a request sound more polite, or to stand-in for *"Do you understand?"* But to the child—a concrete thinker unfamiliar with these blips in the English language—"OK" can sound very much like a question to which the child has the option of saying "yes" or "no." And very likely in his opinion, it is NOT OK that it's time to go to bed.

Asking for agreement is appropriate when the child has a real choice and when you are modeling manners, but when you are *not* offering a choice, ask yourself: is it really OK to use *OK*?

PARENT AND CHILD EMOTIONS

With all that's going on with children aged three to six, parents can feel that raising children comes with a free ride on an emotional roller coaster. Some moments will feel joyful and celebratory, while others feel like a series of frustrations, problems, and unending arguments. It can create a sense of wear and tear that leaves the adult both physically and emotionally exhausted.

Although it can be difficult to keep up with the energy and intensity of the physical play of preschoolers, parents are often more deeply challenged by emotions—their children's and their own.

One way to begin to name the challenge of living with children's emotions is for the parent to explore some of the patterns they may have experienced when growing up. Take a look at what are often called the "Big Four" in the world of emotions: Happy, Mad, Sad, and Scared.

Below are some of the common responses to children exhibiting these emotions, and the potential interpretations children make.

Emotion →	Parents' response →	Children's inner message
Happy High energy state—often loud—running, squealing, jumping, yelling	"Stop it!"	Don't be really happy
	"Take it outside"	Go away! Take your happiness somewhere else
	"Someone's going to get hurt"	Be fearful if things seem to be going too well.

Before we go further it might help to stop and notice two things: First, that parents often respond to children who are really happy and those who are really angry in much the same way. When children are really happy they have a lot of energy—so much so that they may actually be bouncing off the walls, each other, and the furniture! This kind of moving energy usually includes sound—a lot of it and at a volume that can be challenging for parents and sleeping siblings. It is easy to see why parents want it to stop, but here's the catch: do we really want to stop our children from being happy? The answer, of course, is obviously not. More likely what we want is for children to understand when and where to express big muscle excitement and loud sounds, which means parents and children alike would benefit from thinking about where in the home big muscle excitement can be expressed so that everyone can share in a "happy home." IF the child already understands that the place for running, jumping, and big sounds is outside, then "take it outside" isn't a bad message to send. To counter the potential message of "Don't be happy around me," perhaps at least some of the time stressed Mom will go outside with them to share in their happiness.

Emotion	Parents' response	Children's inner message
Mad High energy state— often loud—running, punching, throwing, yelling, growling	"Stop it!"	It is not okay be angry—ever!"
	Go to your room!"	I have to be alone if I'm angry.
	"Stop it or I'll spank you!"	I deserve punishment if I get mad.
	"You'll hurt someone"	I can't trust myself if I get mad.

Most young children will not be able to empathize with a parent who wants a younger sibling to sleep in a quieter environment. Rather than trying to continually remind the child, music can be used as a powerful tool to express physical joy and to provide a consistency to the sound so that younger sleepers can get their rest while older children sing and dance along. When weather is inclement or the space too limited for intense activity, it can be helpful to engage happy children in creating their own small spaces by building houses and stores from sofa pillows or sheets over card tables and chairs. Crawling in, around, and through can be a fun way to spend energy.

Because we carry the reactions and messages from our parents and the environment with us into adulthood, we may carry hidden fears about what it means to be a feeling

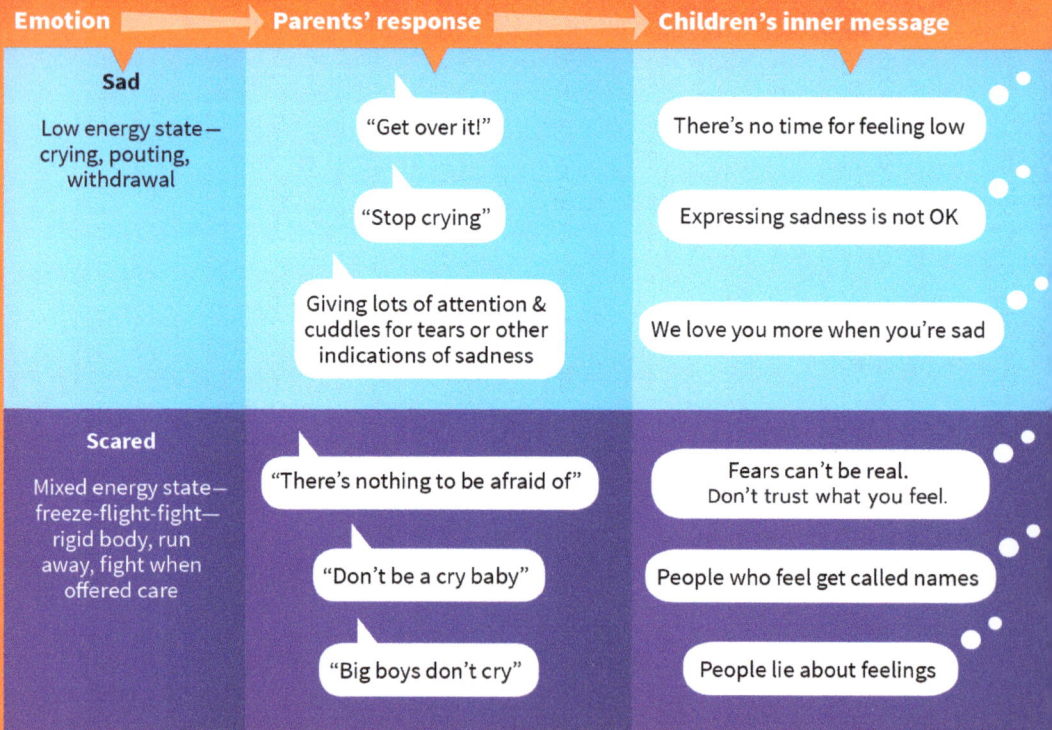

Emotion	Parents' response	Children's inner message
Sad Low energy state—crying, pouting, withdrawal	"Get over it!"	There's no time for feeling low
	"Stop crying"	Expressing sadness is not OK
	Giving lots of attention & cuddles for tears or other indications of sadness	We love you more when you're sad
Scared Mixed energy state—freeze-flight-fight—rigid body, run away, fight when offered care	"There's nothing to be afraid of"	Fears can't be real. Don't trust what you feel.
	"Don't be a cry baby"	People who feel get called names
	"Big boys don't cry"	People lie about feelings

human being. You may have been taught to be embarrassed about your feelings or even made to feel bad about yourself when you have a strong emotional response. So, although culturally we have come to a place where parents can understand and use the phrase, "It is OK to feel," it is often the case that we remain deeply uncertain about what to do in the face of small people with BIG feelings.

The messages parents inadvertently send of which emotions are approved and which are unapproved, along with how to appropriately express them, are confusing! Mom and Dad may yell at sporting events on TV, and yet be angry if siblings yell during disagreements.

Children are concrete thinkers. Even when we think we are being clear, we might be sending mixed messages. Consider the phrasing of the following directions: "It's OK to be mad, but you can't hit your sister."

The concrete thinker may hear this and understand that it is not OK to hit *his sister* when he's mad, but maybe it *is* OK to *hit someone else* when he is mad.

As an adult we respond with a resounding, "Of course not!" But our knowledge is based on a wider range of experiences and contexts that children do not have.

Let's try it another way. Children are often told that a behavior is OK in one setting but not another, for example, "Don't run in the house. Go outside to run." They may then ask, "Is hitting my sister not OK when I'm angry but OK at other times?" The parallel does not work, and without direct teaching, it may take longer for some children to integrate the intended rules for getting along with family and friends.

Meanwhile, parents still struggle to manage their own physical and emotional responses. Our "softer" emotions are often seen as inappropriate in public and work environments. Tears and other expressions of fear, sadness, or disappointment, for example, are rapidly discouraged. For a parent who was taught not to cry or yell, it may be especially difficult to stand in the face of children who are doing just that—at the very top of their voices.

The older toddler and the preschooler are engaged in some pretty intense emotional work. Somewhere, usually between two and a half and three and a half years, the brain has another growth spurt, and with it comes a new developmental task: feelings and how to cope with them. As parents, we coach our children as they develop the skills they need to manage their inner life. This will require some direct teaching about "*What do you do when you feel...*"

For example, the emotion of anger is high energy, and without direct teaching and guidance, the child will naturally resort to hitting, biting, and kicking as natural ways to express her energy. However, this kind of reaction soon becomes a hindrance to relationships with siblings and peers.

HERE ARE SOME OF THE STRATEGIES THAT CAN HELP BOTH PARENTS AND CHILDREN

Teach a feeling vocabulary! We, as a culture, can hardly speak the language of feelings. When was the last time you heard an adult say he or she felt anything beyond happy, sad, or mad? Many of us have no idea how limited our feeling vocabulary is until we explore the variety of words related to feelings. For instance, when was the last time you used the word effervescent to describe the almost bubbly feeling of happiness?

Teaching this kind of vocabulary through everyday interactions can look like this:

- "I see a boy who feels (delighted, pleased, proud, thrilled, terrific) about his Halloween costume."

- "I see my two boys feeling (content, relaxed, peaceful, tranquil) in their reading pillows."

- "It looks like right now you feel (demoralized, disappointed, sorrowful; furious, frustrated, displeased, annoyed, provoked) because Momma had to remind you that it is time to stop playing."

- "It looks as though you are feeling (tense, uneasy, upset, uptight, unsure, worried) about going to preschool."

(For more suggestions see *The ABCs of a Feeling Vocabulary,* page 36.)

Watch your child's biology! Be aware of when and how many choices the child must make in a day. For instance, in thinking about the "when":

- Making a breakfast choice may be too hard on a hungry tummy.

- Choosing books at bedtime may be too much for a tired body and brain.

- Choosing a shirt may be extra challenging when there is a rush to get out the door in time.

Support the development of physical impulse control. Physical impulse control requires that children be able to stop their bodies. Play activities that require children to stop their bodies when they're having fun (remember that happiness is a high-energy state) contribute to children's ability to stop their body in other intense-feeling moments. Whether the game is simple and music-based like a toddler's game of "Ring around the Rosie," or preschool children playing freeze tag and needing to respond to a tap on the shoulder, children learn how to bring their bodies under intentional control through play. As a side benefit, when adults play along we support a sense of shared family joy and also build fitness activity into daily life.

Use books! Go to your children's librarian and ask for recommendations on books about feelings. You will find there are books with stories of characters who work through the fear of going to school; being mad at little siblings; getting through a friendship squabble; and a variety of other social-emotional difficulties preschool children face. Before you share the new book with your child, make sure to pre-read the books you've chosen. And remember that children tend to identify with the main character of the book. If you like the way the main character approaches the problem, then introduce the book to your young problem-solver.

Remember that a picture is worth a thousand words! For example, *No, David* is a picture book in which David does a number of "bad" things. The book's refrain is, *No, David!* For a late preschooler or older child, these are funny because they have already internalized many of the appropriate rules and can feel superior to David who "just doesn't get it." However, the ability to hold the negative mental image in contrast to the positive behavior may be developmentally impossible for some. *For many young children, if they see a picture of what NOT to do, that is the picture that will hold their focus and be more influential than the words.*

Plan for some fun with your child! Rather than setting yourself up as the ruler of everything, spend some time in the day where your child can direct some shared play. This means they get to pick whether you play cars or build blocks. They will be the one to tell you where the yellow car is parked and how it needs to drive around the corner. This is not the time to teach them anything about whether cars can fly. They are the controller of the play. If you can't stand playing cars, set a timer for how long you can share your "magic time when they are the boss of the world."

Keep learning and take care of yourself! We are lifelong learners. Unfortunately, some of what we learn as adults is that we must un-learn or adapt some of our understanding from our childhood. This is particularly true when faced with learning about managing emotions. When relating to children, fathers may be especially distressed by their son's tears, while mothers may find dealing with children's anger the greater challenge, based on their early learning about when and how to express emotions.

Not only may the learning be incomplete, but it may actually be limiting our ability to maintain our important adult relationships. Men who have been taught not to express their softer emotions of care can be criticized as adults for not being emotionally supportive of the women and children in their lives. Women who may have been told they were bad if they expressed anger or disappointment may attempt to hold emotions in check until they become explosive or depressive.

Helping children learn to live with emotions is hard work. Share these challenges with a loved one or trusted friend who will not judge you for thinking aloud or feel as though they need to take a side between you and your child. Share time with families who can model strategies that you would like to practice in your home. Take time away for yourself—individually and, when possible, as a couple. You may choose to spend time with others or do something that feels like fun to you. These moments for self and couples allow adults an opportunity to maintain a sense of energy for life (that inner child joy), without ignoring the responsibilities and challenges of maturity. Remember that no matter how grown up *we* are, *they* will keep us growing if we pay attention to ourselves too.

TANTRUMS

Parents may be surprised that children who did not particularly have tantrums at age two may begin to have them during the preschool years. There are three core guidelines for adults who stand in the face of children's intense physical reactions.

During a tantrum, you may not:

- Hurt yourself

- Hurt any other person/animal

- Harm things of value to the family or in the shared living environment

The guidelines define the nature of intervention adults offer when children are overwhelmed or struggling to manage their bodies and their feelings. As children continue to grow, adult interventions shift and engage children more in meeting expectations for their own self-regulation.

When children experience significant difficulty in self-regulation, the whole village of family, school, and healthcare may be called upon for guidance and support. In some instances, identifying allergies, implementing change in eating and sleep routines, or addressing learning difficulties can ease biological and social stress, which results in successful self-regulation at home and school.

THE CHILD IS NOT A SHORT ADULT

The child's body cannot manage lack of food, lack of sleep, or a hurried schedule as well as an adult body (which does not necessarily manage these stressors all that easily, either). The child has not yet developed the internal resources that adults use every day. For instance, imagine an adult and a child standing in line. Both are bored and impatient. The adult understands time. She can remind herself why she is standing in line, or calm herself with the thought that later she will go on a run. The child lives in the moment. He is without the simple coping strategies that adults often take for granted. In addition, movement is so much a part of the child's life that any activity that restricts moving is often more challenging than it would seem to adults.

TANTRUMS (THROUGH THE AGES)

Toddler	Preschooler ~3-6	K+ ~6-8
May have minimal language	Learning to use language to problem solve	Must use language to problem solve
Immature central nervous system which overloads easily when tired, hungry, etc.	Maturing central nervous system which may continue to need to be watched for overload	Expect regular routines to buffer physical stressors of hunger and sleep needs
Expect no impulse control	Expect to see beginning development of impulse control	More independent peer to peer social activity requires that children will self-limit behavior
No language to express feelings	Developing vocabulary of feelings	Rarely able to be self-reflective in reporting why they reacted. (Self-reflection usually develops mid-elementary)

STRATEGIES

Toddler	Preschooler ~3-6	K+ ~6-8
Adult's responsibility to maintain safety for child and others	Adult's responsibility to maintain safety; but child can begin to integrate limits on behavior, e.g., no hitting	Children are expected to be active participants in maintaining safety during conflicts or when faced with disappointment
Adults learn children's patterns of eating and sleep needs to "Head it off at the pass"	Heading "it" off may work on occasion, but plan strategies for teaching/coaching children on what to do with their bodies when there are big feelings	Complex social learning environments—school, home, sports—engage multiple adults with expectations and in teaching self-regulation
Calm and soothe as needed	Empathize with feelings before guiding behavior!	Add logical consequences and atonement tasks when children fail to manage interactions with others and the environment.
Routine, routine, routine	Verbally prepare children for change, offer tools for managing disappointment, anger, fear, etc.	Continue to coach strategies until they are integrated into behavioral reactions

WHEN WE HAVE A WORRIER

Every child will experience situations that take them by surprise and may create some level of anxiety. After all, from preschool age on, my growing brain can make comparisons and I've realized the world is huge! Furthermore, we live in a culture that has many opportunities, but as such, often sets a pace that is hectic even for adults. Even the most outgoing and energetic children will sometimes find such a world challenging.

When a child experiences worry that lasts beyond the circumstances of an occasional event, we need to offer them very concrete strategies to manage their fear and anxiety next time it occurs. This will help them to manage their anxiety in the moment, and to build skills that can be applied to a number of life experiences. These are skills that contribute to a lifetime of emotional resilience.

At a time when not in the fear situation: Talk about how to address the worry the next time it comes up. Young children often express their anxiety as fear of being alone. Until confident of your presence, they are unlikely to be able to hear how to manage if you were not available. Therefore, you should discuss, in concrete terms, who the child can seek help from (make sure you discuss

Help children be calm enough to learn. When the stress hormone cortisol floods the brain it makes it much harder to learn! People of every size learn best when they are engaged to the level of interest, but not pushed into overwhelm mode.

. . . .

Parents will sometimes hand a phone to a child to play games or use as a distractor, and fail to teach them how to use it for their own safety. Does your child know how to call another trusted adult and when and how to use 911 in an emergency?

multiple possible helpers), how the child would reach them, and particularly in a 911 emergency what they should say. After you have talked about the worry and given them strategies, you can expect that for a few weeks children will continue to need reinforcement. For example, a panicked call of "Mom! Where are you?" can be met with, "I'm right here. Remember you don't have to worry. If you couldn't find me, you would call Aunt Janet and she would help you."

INCREASE SELF-CARE SKILLS

For food preparation, use child-size containers. Children cannot yet understand volume and will continue to pour beyond the level of a glass.

- Dressing is often the first self-care skill that parents support.

- Simple snack/meal preparation—for example, a sandwich—should also be one of the child's skills.

- Safely getting a glass of water or pouring milk.

  ○ For this kind of practice, use small pitchers so there is not a lot of spillage.

- Place clear limits on the kinds of things to practice in different environments.

  ○ For example: in the kitchen, the microwave, stove, and sharp knives are off limits!

EMOTIONAL LEARNING STRATEGIES

Practice self-calming strategies in a variety of settings. These can be practiced across a variety of feelings, including positive ones, such as when a child is physically bursting with happiness but needs to slow their body down to suit the social context. Some children can be encouraged to find their favorite blanket or lovey to self-calm at a too-busy event. Or they could ask Dad to come and stand with them until their body is less worried.

Teach basic self-assertion skills. This can be as simple as teaching phrases like, "I need a minute to do it myself," or, "Please, let's not hurry."

Teach how to focus on the positives. When children seem to be building a pattern of focusing on the negative, insist that they tell you one good thing, then they can tell their bad thing. Close by sandwiching that thought with one other good thing.

CATCH YOUR CHILD BEING BRAVE AND RESOURCEFUL!

Sometimes we focus so much on the child when they are struggling that we forget to acknowledge their steps along the way. When they are successful in small ways and we acknowledge it, we help them gain confidence that they can handle this great wide world before them.

THE ABCS OF A FEELING VOCABULARY

A is for acceptance, admired, adored, affectionate, aggravated, alarmed, alert, ambivalent, amused, animated, angry, annoyed, antagonistic, anticipating, anxious, apathetic, appalled, appealing, appreciated, apprehensive, ashamed, assured, astonished, audacious, awkward, and awed. Do you know more?

B is for bashful, belligerent, benevolent, bewildered, bold, bored, bothered, bubbly, buoyant, brave, bright, and brash.

C is for calm, carefree, cared-for, cautious, cocky, competent, concerned, confident, comfortable, confused, consoled, contemptuous, cornered, covetous, crushed, curious, and cynical.

D is for daring, defeated, degraded, dejected, delighted, dependent, depressed, despairing, desperate, despised, devastated, disappointed, disapproval, disconcerted, disconsolate, discouraged, disgruntled, disgusted, dislike, dismal, dismayed, dissatisfied, distrustful, disturbed, doubtful, dour, down, and dread.

E is for eager, edgy, elated, embarrassed, empathetic, enraged, envious, esteemed, estranged, exasperated, excited, exhausted, and expectant.

F is for fearful, fed up, fond, forlorn, frantic, friendly, frightened, fulfilled, furious, futile, and ferocious.

G is for glad, gleeful, gloomy, good, grateful, great, grieved, grouchy, grumpy, and guilty.

H is for happy, hapless, hateful, helpless, hopeful, hopeless, horrified, hostile, humbled, humiliated, and hurt.

I is for impatient, important, idolized, inadequate, independent, indifferent, indignant, ineffectual, infatuated, inferior, inhibited, inquisitive, irritated, insecure, and insulted.

J is for joyful, jealous, jittery, jolly, judicious, justified, and jumpy.

K is for klutzy, kind, and kittenish.

L is for lethargic, listless, loathed, lonely, longing, lost, loving, loved, and loyal.

M is for mad, meaningless, melancholy, merry, miserable, mistrustful, mixed-up, and moody.

N is for nervous, nonplused, and nosy.

O is for optimistic, out of sorts, outraged, and overwhelmed.

P is for pained, panicked, passionate, patient, peaceful, perplexed, persistent, pessimistic, pitiful, pleased, pressured, proud, provoked, put-down, and puzzled.

Q is for quirky, quixotic, and quizzical.

R is for refreshed, regretful, rejected, relaxed, relieved, reluctant, repulsed, resentful, resigned, and restless.

S is for sad, satisfied, scared, self-conscious, sexy, shocked, shy, skeptical, solemn, sorry, startled, strong, stubborn, sullen, supported, surprised, suspicious, and sympathetic.

T is for teed-off, tender, tense, tempted, threatened, thrilled, timid, torn-up, tough, tranquil, trapped, trepidation, troubled, trusting, turned off, and turned on.

U is for uncomfortable, uneasy, unfulfilled, unhappy, unsure, untroubled, unwanted, upbeat, upset, uptight, used, and useless.

V is for valiant, valued, vibrant, vivacious, vital, and vulnerable.

W is for warm, weak, weary, wondering, worn out, worried, worthless, worthy, wounded, and wrung out.

X is for feeling left out and unwanted.

Y is for yearning and youthful.

Z is for zealous and zany.

HOW THE REMOTE CAN TEACH YOUR CHILD SELF-CONTROL

If there are screens in your house, your pocket, or your purse, screens will be a part of your child's life. This reality brings with it many conflicts and justifiable concerns, so it's nice to be able to add something, however small, that is positive.

We don't often analyze what we are called to do to be successful with our day-to-day interactions with one another, but certainly one basic element is the ability to regulate our bodies. For better or for worse, many young children have mastered the use of the remote control. They've also mastered the logic of it: they know what it means to play, pause, stop, and rewind. Why not use that to your advantage?

Using the remote as an analogy for body regulation is a perfect match for their hand-eye real-world knowledge, as well as the concrete thinking skills of their young minds.

In some schools, teachers have used the model of the remote as a social skill teaching tool. The remote-control analogy works at home too: a STOP button for self-control, the PAUSE button to reflect on the action, a chance to REWIND to make the interaction with the friend better, and then a return to PLAY.

With the familiar image of the TV remote as a guide, the child can learn to:

• Hit that red STOP button within his body.

• PAUSE to give himself time to breathe, self-calm, and take control of his mouth and his muscles. The PAUSE also provides opportunity for a preschool child to see the outcome of his actions (his friends' tears, a spill) and to plan his response.

• REWIND to the decision point and make another choice in an attempt to improve the outcome for himself and those around him. (Do something to help his friend, find the cloth to wipe up the spill.)

• Resume the PLAY, perhaps by atoning or bringing his age-appropriate negotiation skills to problem-solve.

Many children hear "stop" and "no" all day. But by moving beyond a simple STOP and focusing on PAUSE and REWIND, we're ultimately teaching children the value of finding ways to make it better.

Playing games in which STOP is an important element, such as freeze tag, can help children have fun with the concept. Also, remember to celebrate success when a child has been successful with "pausing" and "rewinding," by noting a successful playdate or interaction with a sibling. Some families will build these reflections on the day's success stories into their bedtime routine.

SOCIAL-
EMOTIONAL

The term "social-emotional" (or, as some prefer, psycho-social) is a compound word used to represent the complex work that we humans do as we develop. Let's break it down.

The social component refers to the learning we do about others and ourselves through our interactions. An individual's social context can include everything from family interactions, including any labeling, to the physical spaces that comprise our homes and neighborhoods. Our social context helps shape the individuals we become.

The emotional and psycho (logical) component refers to our inner sense of who we are, which changes and develops over time. This might be expressed by questions such as: Do I feel cared for? What feelings do I have related to labels that have been assigned to me (such as bad, smart, or strong)? Do the kids in class like me?

Since social-emotional development includes what we do in interaction with others, as well as what we feel, adults support children's development not only through providing their love and care, but also through teaching and coaching. Adults can teach children skills that help them manage the complexity of social life, and coach them to develop coping strategies that support a positive inner experience of self and world.

Let's think about the social world of a child. When an adult says, "What's the magic word?" most of us anticipate that the child will respond with "please." This is a common scenario that is part of a cultural pattern we have in place for teaching children the basics of social interactions. The common term for this kind of interaction is "manners." (In this case it is short for the manner in which to ask.) When everyone in a given social situation knows and uses socially defined manners, interactions are smoother and tensions decrease. Along with the ABCs and 123s, preschool children are expected to learn social manners that will serve them at home and in the classroom.

Basic classroom manners require that children become skilled in a variety of interactions. For instance, to be skilled at using classroom manners children must be able to read the context of the interaction and choose a response that reflects and communicates their understanding. Consider the following list of independent social encounters a child may have in a classroom:

- Greeting a classmate

- Saying "thank you"

- Responding to a "thank you"

- Learning to ask for help from an adult or a classmate

- Asking someone to play

- Following the rules of a game

- Offering help

- Taking turns talking

- Taking turns with equipment

- Paying attention to the words of an adult leader

- Paying attention to the words of another child

Many of us take these skills for granted, forgetting that at one point each of us was a beginner. Further, we may forget that the sheer number of skills there are means that we are very likely to be better at some of them than others. With any learning, children may develop different skills at different rates.

Social skills require a high level of physical self-regulation and internalization of the values of the social context. We hope that children experience joy at their accomplishments and in budding friendships, and gain satisfaction from trying when things get hard. We know they will also experience some less than pleasant feelings—disappointment about not being first or at losing a game, or anger at being told "no" or "not right now." Accepting the consequences of one's choices is hard work. While we may think a child's concerns are trivial, in developmental terms they are monumental. They provide the practice through which children learn to see themselves in relationship to others and to manage their feelings.

Children will begin to report perceived personal injustices across their social domains—a missed turn to be first in a classroom line, a sibling who used their toy without asking, a friend who got a new toy or special snack. These (seemingly petty to the adult) issues indicate more awareness of the world and a budding moral code. Parental empathy related to the feelings underlying these reports creates a framework for trust between child and adult. Remember, someday we will want our teens to come to us for important issues. These are the issues that are important to them now.

Along with the social component, there is the great challenge of creating a context of personal and emotional safety in early classrooms. For example, to successfully manage in a classroom, children must be able to:

- Deal with feeling mad (a high-energy state in which increased stress hormones flood the brain)

- Restrain from hitting others (applying the value of individual safety)

- Calm themselves (lower the stress hormones)

- Shift from reacting with their bodies to using cognitive skills and words to problem-solve

Some children will need the resources of a supportive adult to manage emotional intensity (the adult should remember the trifecta: relax/calm/reassure) so that the child can use cognitive skills and words to resolve issues. Having calmed a child, the adult may need to directly teach what the next steps are to resolve the issue. For example, a disappointed child can be reminded that her turn to be line leader was last week and that another turn will come. Then she may be invited to join the line near one of her special friends (emotional support is one tool in learning to cope with disappointment).

Just as rituals and routines help to manage the flow in a home, they are equally valuable in learning environments. (See *The Preschool Decision*, page 135.) Children soon come to trust that emotional upsets will be fairly resolved—the prior disappointment about being line leader is buffered by expectation that, although delayed at this moment, opportunity to be line leader is assured. As they learn to anticipate the flow of the day, they begin to experience less stress around transitions. This allows children to be free to expand further on the social skills that underlie the academic curriculum, such as: learning when and how to interrupt to ask a question; learning when it's time to follow directions and when it's time to choose from options; learning when it's time to work in a group and when it's time to practice independent learning. Even learning what to ignore and how to ignore it is a social skill. It takes practice to go from the snuggled, shared focus of reading with a parent to reading during a story circle when they must ignore the wiggles of their classmate.

IN TROUBLE AT SCHOOL

No parent looks forward to a call from school about a child's behavior problem. When a call comes, it can bring memories of a parent's own negative childhood experiences with teachers or classmates, a sense of fear that their child somehow *is* a problem versus the important distinction that they simply *have* a problem at the moment, or the instinctive impulse to "defend our own" no matter the circumstance. Unfortunately, none of these stances are helpful to children, parents, or teachers.

It is important to remember that a parent's childhood history is not the child's present.

Parent experiences—childhood and adult—shape expectations of places and people. If a history of school or relationships with teachers felt negative, it could taint the ability to support children in issues arising from school. It may not be easy, but if at all possible, being aware of the emotional baggage we may carry from our own school experience is important. On the flip side, parents who experienced few if any social challenges in school could be unnecessarily embarrassed or feel a sense of personal failure if a child's behavior triggers a call from school.

By attaining clarity about the separation between your own past and your child's present, you can better begin to problem-solve.

Keep in mind that children are captive audiences in school, and they do not possess the autonomy that adults often have to leave a situation if it is unpleasant.

Instead, they may express their discomfort through unexplained tummy aches, increased tantrums, or negative behavior at home. When parents see shifts in their children's behavior it may be time to take a step back and explore more than their immediate physical ailments. The issue may require more information about the environment or social demands during the day. (See *Family Advisor*s, page 107, for prompts to help you.)

THERE'S TROUBLE AND THEN THERE'S *TROUBLE*

An occasional dustup between peers that is quickly resolved is usually a normal part of growing up, no matter how awkward it may feel to parents. To determine if specific support or intervention is needed, one may need to consider how *often* "trouble" occurs and how *intense* it is.

When the learning environment is being disrupted for the child and/or others, "trouble" can point to a social-emotional learning need. There are categories of social-emotional skills to consider. Some fall into a range of school-related skills that can include the following:

- Asking questions and being able to use the answers
- Following directions, individually and in a group
- Completing a task, even when it seems uninteresting or difficult
- Knowing when and how to interrupt to ask for help

Other social-emotional skills center around successful peer interactions, particularly those that support making and maintaining friendships:

- Greeting others
- Reading others
- Knowing how to join in play
- Waiting for and offering turns
- Offering or receiving help
- Inviting another to play

- Showing affection
- Recognizing their own feelings and the feelings of others (empathy may not develop until middle elementary)

Still others are skills children can employ to help themselves manage or avoid aggression:

- Self-calming
- Determining if something is fair
- Saying "no" to protect personal boundaries
- Knowing when to tell an adult
- Deciding what to do rather than acting impulsively

Keeping in mind the various types of social-emotional tasks that children must learn can help parents and other adults analyze peer- and school-related trouble, and more specifically, target skills needed for success.

PLAYMATES: FROM SHADOWING TO COACHING

Developmentally, toddlers and preschoolers need help to play with one another. When they are first beginning to play with others, the adult can practice shadowing (staying physically near) in order to:

- Interpret a playmate's immature attempts to engage a friend

- Ensure that neither child is hurt

- Teach directly how to take turns

- Support speech development by supplying words to actions and objects

- Monitor the pace and intensity of the play

For children with quieter temperaments, having an adult shadow them may mean the difference between enjoying being in a group and displaying anxious behaviors like clinging. For children with high-intensity temperaments, it may mean the difference between learning quickly to manage peer boundaries and becoming difficult for peers to enjoy.

In general, adults can expect to shadow children under the age of three. However, as preschool children grow, they continue to integrate emotional regulation, and develop more physical and social skills. Hence, they will require less immediate support from adults. There is a natural progression from the need for shadowing toward coaching more complex levels of play. For adults to shift from shadowing to coaching it may help to understand what it takes to be a good coach in any area.

To coach, one must:

- **Know the rules of the game.**

- **Recognize the players as learners who have a variety of skills.**

- **Analyze the current skill level of the player.**

- **Provide both an appropriate safe place to practice and ample time for practice.**

Shadowing OR Coaching

Shadowing

Using your words to give meaning to another child's approach.

> It looks like Sam wants to see what you're playing with.

Placing your body between children to maintain safety.

> I'm moving to the front of the slide so that I can help your friends remember to leave room for you to come down.

Becoming the other player.

> You know what? It looks like you want to use muscles too big for your friend. Let's go run over here.

Actually entering the play group activity to help manage the logistics of space and turn taking.

> Everyone is busy cooking today. It looks like George wants lids on all the pans. Let's find some dishes that don't need lids so our fingers are not in the way.

Coaching

Encouraging children to use their words.

> Tell Sally you aren't done yet.

Defining the limits of their play.

> The place for running is on the grass not the patio where your baby sister is playing.

Being calm in the face of their emotional struggles with one another. (Your physical presence allows them to co-regulate with you so that they can co-regulate with one another.)

> I'll keep you company while you figure out something both of you want to play.

Insisting that children honor social rules and one another's boundaries.

> I know you wanted to use your brother's toy. Because it's his, he gets to decide when you can play with it.

Notice the developmental differences and the strategies used in shadowing and coaching children at play.

Preschoolers are in the Social Skill Peewee League. It will become increasingly apparent when children can be expected to play more easily with one another and which combinations of temperament and physical energy will require more support and coaching. Older preschool children may need less coaching, but there will continue to be times during which it will help children to have a supportive adult near as they become more sophisticated social problem-solvers. Remember, parents who are too quick to resolve conflicts about turns, or who step in to negotiate roles in creative play, may unintentionally deny children the opportunity to build their skills and self-confidence through practice. It is important for adults to remember that they are coaching and not playing the game for the children involved!

Here is a quick overview of the most common things children will fight about, the expected developmental skills and limitations that children have to manage conflict at each stage, and the leadership demands on the adults who are their models and guides.

Age/Stage	Infant & Toddler	Preschooler	Kindergarten+
Nature of Conflict	• Caregiver Interaction • Objects	• Who's in charge! • Initial boundary disputes • Attention	• Boundaries • Early justice/fairness issues • Rules: what, when, how, who enforces them • Attention
Child Developmental Limitations and Skills	• No Impulse Control • Receptive Language: can understand tone and some contextual speech from an adult caregiver • Cannot understand that they could injure a playmate • Need for co-regulation with adult • Trust in adults to help keep them calm and safe	• Developing Impulse Control • Expressive language: can use speech to report • Cannot separate fantasy from reality • Cannot yet consistently read the intent of the other • Can begin to contribute suggestions for how to resolve conflicts • Expects adult involvement and may seek it to win in a conflict • May benefit from co-regulation with adult to maintain calm while thinking about conflict	• Moderate Impulse control • Moderate emotional self-regulation • Expanding understanding of rules • Will engage adults for help • May need adults to insist they practice problem solving with strategies other than physical strength
Adult Roles and Skills that help children manage conflict	• Do most of the work • Provide physical boundaries for safety • Shadow • Translate intent of other child • Introduce turn taking	• Ensure physical safety • Teach the rules of engagement! "You may not hit!" "Use your words!" • Teach a feeling vocabulary • Insist that children read social cues and begin to actively participate in resolution • Model values, avoid labels like good and bad • Support turn taking	• Teach values with direct language & supplement with value literature • Expect to hear, "But that's not fair!" • Teach and play games that have rules • Help children keep calm when the game does not go their way • Teach that "losing" is not being a "loser" or devalued in any way • Teach the difference between assertion and aggression

SIBLINGS: BLESSING AND BANE

The chart included in the section on shadowing gives an overview of children learning social engagement with peers. But, for parents, unless children are womb-mates, siblings are rarely at the same developmental stage. And even when they are, there are some stages in which self-regulation and social skills are so limited that conflict with the potential for physical injury will be a part of every day.

In general, when infants, toddlers, and preschool-age children play together, adult supervision is needed—for safety and enjoyment. The human face is so interesting to infants and toddlers, in particular, that small fingers will quickly go to the face of the other child. When crawling, the other's body is just one more obstacle to get over. Preschoolers have so little impulse control, and have gotten so much bigger and stronger, that running and bumping are a given part of every day. The self-regulation to determine how big a hug to give to baby brother or sister is rarely in place at this stage and requires that parents never assume an infant's safety when preschool and toddler siblings are left alone with them.

Once children have basic impulse control and know the safety rules of play, there are general strategies parents can use to help make sibling issues a chance for children to grow as individuals and to support their relationship skills.

Be clear about your family values and the goals you have for your children

No family can be conflict-free, but parents define the rules about how to manage fights to keep everyone safe and help the children remain friends. A basic framework of the rules that work in many families include prohibitions on physical retaliation, rules about ownership, and rules for turn taking.

Be clear about the difference between feelings and actions

Although parents want to have their children grow up to love and care for one another, confusing the feelings in the moment with the long-term relationship is not helpful. Simple phrases help children clarify the responsibility to manage their inner lives as well as their bodies. For example, if the child says, *"But I don't like her!"* you could respond, *"You don't have to like your sister, but you may not hit her."*

Do not problem-solve for your children

If children cannot work together without someone being hurt, your presence will be important for them to stay safe. That does not mean you become judge, jury, and law enforcement in each of their disagreements. You know you have slipped into one of those roles when you hear yourself say:

"Who started it?"

"He didn't mean it."

"Stop fighting or I'll take it from both of you."

Help children understand when they *do* need an adult to problem-solve

In some instances, especially where safety is involved, the children will need support to have an adult intervene. Help them to understand that there is a difference between "tattling" to gain power in a conflict with a sibling, and telling an adult when someone is doing something that is dangerous. Some children will attempt to engage adults many times until this distinction becomes clear. Out in the world, preschool children will often report when they see others breaking a rule from home. Do expect to hear comments like, "He isn't holding his mom's hand." To which you can respond, "Are you proud that you remember how we do it to stay safe?"

Notice when and where conflicts take place

If children only fight when they are too tired to cope, they may need help to take a break or find some quiet activity away from siblings. If they only fight in confined spaces like the car, they may need help to manage their energy level before they have to be together in small spaces; for longer trips it may mean that adults budget time to let them jump around or have a race at the rest stops. Or, if they fight when one or the other is bored, they may need to find ways to entertain themselves. In a vehicle there are options like travel games, music, or other electronics. When at home it may be time to explore creative projects.

The need for attention

Consider whether your children fight more when you have the most work to do, have to spend a long time on the phone, or have a family crisis that has you more distracted than usual. For parents who work from home, it may be wise to engage childcare during work hours. When there is significant family stress, it may help to engage friends and other supportive people who are able to offer additional attention until the crisis has passed. For children who are seeking attention it can be helpful to notice and acknowledge them when they are quiet and happy together. Most parents would like their children to have the attention they *need*. If their attention quota is met, children do not need negative behaviors to seek parents' engagement.

Remember where they are developmentally

Children's sense of fairness and justice grows as they are better able to understand another's point of view and to enter into problem-solving that considers their own needs and wants as well as another's needs and wants. You can expect to hear children who are near six years old say, *"But that's not fair!"*

Finally, note whether the expectations that are placed on the children would ever be applied to adults

Here are some phrases that may indicate an unrealistic expectation during sibling conflicts:

"You weren't using it." The words may very well be true; however, few car owners would be consoled to hear this from a policeman after their car was stolen from a mall. Even though the owner wasn't technically using it at that moment, the reality is that community systems work better for everyone when there is respect for ownership. At home, children may want very much to explore the toys and tools of their siblings. Teaching children to ask permission, to deal with feelings of disappointment, and to experience the satisfaction of granting another a favor are some of the gifts of resolving sibling conflicts while honoring boundaries and ownership.

"Give it to him; he's littler than you." Again, it may be true that the other sibling in the conflict is smaller. As an adult, though, one can only imagine the chaos that team sports would be if the smallest contenders were always given the ball. Having rules for positive engagement with others no matter what their size supports younger children as they are learning the rules of ownership and boundaries, and older children as they are learning to resist physically hurting others who are smaller and weaker.

Sibling relationships are usually the longest relationships adults ever have. Whether those relationships develop as lifelong blessings is in part shaped by the efforts of parents to lay a framework of rules—rules that honor boundaries, rules that protect, and rules that coach children daily about how to live with others.

PART II:
THE PARENT

PARENTING STYLES

Attachment is everything to the very young. From positive attachment grows positive discipline, positive empathy, and long-term positive relationships. Parenting style is key to the development and maintenance of attachment...or the lack thereof.

"Parenting style" is a broad term that attempts to categorize the behaviors and interactions most often used in discipline and care. Although the tasks of raising children are varied, it has become broadly accepted that the tasks fall into two distinct categories called by a variety of names: Love and Discipline, Warmth and Control, Nurture and Structure. Whatever the name, Love, Warmth, Nurture, are parent behaviors that bring emotional safety and comfort. These parent behaviors are balanced by guidance and teaching strategies—Discipline, Control, Structure—which help children learn the rules of life related to self-care and interactions with others.

Placing these categories into a graph depicting greater and lesser levels of this balancing act results in four broad parenting styles.

Rigid — **Autocratic**	Rigid/Autocratic parenting is a pattern of interaction in which adults respond in ways that the child experiences as harsh, unpredictable, or frightening—creating a context of tentative attachment. Depending on temperament, children react as though the world is a place in which one must freeze, hide or fight. Within this context it is increasingly difficult for children to be secure in the belief that they are loved, as well as trust that the world is a safe place to explore.
Uninvolved — **Neglectful** — **Distracted**	Uninvolved/Neglectful/Distracted parenting of preschool children places children at risk of becoming emotionally unattached to their caregivers. This creates a context in which children do not trust adults to offer emotional or physical support for the challenges of growing and interacting with others. Because preschool children have more strength and skills, their activities may result in injury to mind and spirit, as well as body.

Indulgent ―――― **Laissez-faire** ―――― **Lenient**	Indulgent/Laissez-faire/Lenient parenting of preschool children places both parent and child at risk of "too much of a good thing." Parents who are giving beyond their personal or emotional reserves may begin to resent how little time and energy are "left over" for self-care or couple care. Doing for children what they should be learning to do for themselves takes away the opportunity to learn to be competent. Further, the normal developmental ego-centrism of preschool children needs to be gently challenged to support greater social skills, awareness of their own behavior and to help them cultivate the seeds of responsible ownership.
Authoritative ―――― **Democratic**	Authoritative/Democratic parenting of preschool children is the context in which secure attachment is maintained. Further, it is the context in which children become aware of their impact on others, begin to internalize social patterns based on parent values and begin to trust themselves as competent problem solvers. Authoritative parenting creates an emotional climate in which to thrive.

As noted in the earlier Introduction, all of the advice and information offered in this book is centered in the Authoritative/Democratic quadrant. Lest there be any confusion, in a family with two parents and three children, it does not mean that the children are in charge through majority rule! "Democratic" as used here refers to the power of one's "voice" in the parent-child dyad. For vulnerable children, their "voice" is primarily the parent's understanding of the child's developmental stage—including their immature thinking and planning ability, their lack of impulse control, and appropriate expectations of skills that need to be acquired during this stage of their development. To a lesser degree, a collaborative and respectful adult may find that a child's spoken voice can offer fresh ideas for collaboration with peers and adults.

Loving our children can nudge us to reflect on how we were loved as children. This reflection, when we take it on, can become a powerful path to understanding who we are as parents, as well as who we want to be and how we might get there. The parenting styles chart is a useful tool for thinking about the parenting that you received, and perhaps to better understand others in your life. For some, knowing the power of a parenting style can be reassuring in the face of opinions of friends and extended family whose patterns you can now understand more fully. Others may use

PARENTING STYLES

Rigid/Autocratic

POSSIBLE BELIEF SYSTEM:
I'm the parent, I decide.

WHAT IT CAN LOOK LIKE AT THIS AGE:
- Ongoing invitations to power struggles
- Harsh verbal interactions
- Threats to withdraw support: *If you don't, I won't.*
- Threats of physical violence: *If you continue, I'll spank you.*

PARENT CAN BE:
- Dismissive of child's feelings
- Unaware of child's perspective
- Unaccommodating of child's developmental stage

Authoritative/Democratic

POSSIBLE BELIEF SYSTEM:
Everyone in this family counts. My job is to love, coach, and guide.

WHAT IT CAN LOOK LIKE AT THIS AGE:
- Free cuddles & smiles
- Rhythm to the day
- Acknowledgment rather than praise: *I saw you on the climber, are you proud?*
- Clear, direct teaching about rules
- Clear context to practice decision-making *It's so cold your feet will need another layer. Do you want to choose socks or tights?*
- Reminders of behavior choices with natural & logical consequences when appropriate.

PARENT CAN BE:
- Firm, but not rigid
- Respectful
- Cooperative
- Freely affectionate
- Aware of adult and child needs/wants

MORE CONTROL

LESS WARMTH

MORE WARMTH

Uninvolved/Distracted

POSSIBLE BELIEF SYSTEM:
Kids don't count as much as adults
OR
Kids are often in the way.

WHAT IT CAN LOOK LIKE AT THIS AGE:
- Lack of physical/emotional order to the day
- Meals when it's convenient for mom/dad
- Active or indirect ignoring
- Sending children outside without adult supervision or engagement
- Parental over-engagement with phone or other forms of social media instead of child
- Children "problem solve" without adult coaching for sibling/peer safety
- Childcare inconsistent; sometimes not safe

PARENT CAN:
- Relinquish decision-making
- Relinquish discipline to other adults/older siblings
- Run hot & cold about sharing affection
- Be on-again, off-again about family rules

Indulgent/Lax

POSSIBLE BELIEF SYSTEM:
I'm a good parent when my child is happy.

WHAT IT CAN LOOK LIKE AT THIS AGE:
- Few rules imposed on the child (potential parent martyr)
- Meals/bedtime when it's convenient for child
- No consistent adult-only time
- Praise for Everything!
- Child's things dominate the family space
- Child's wants dominate the family energy
- Overwhelming attention
- Child is never/rarely inconvenienced

PARENT CAN:
- Be easily openly affectionate
- Have difficulty saying No
- Use bribery to avoid conflict
- Be unaware of adult needs

LESS CONTROL

a discussion of temperament (see *Temperament Matters, page 59*) and parenting styles to adapt or expand strategies in guiding children.

There is considerable research on the effects of parenting style. These outcomes are, of course, influenced by other factors, one of which is temperament. As an example: children who have experienced Rigid/Autocratic parenting are at risk of being withdrawn or overly compliant, *and* they are also at a greater risk of rebellious and defiant behavior. These opposite outcomes reflect innate differences in temperament that would have one child turn inward and the other more outward in response to parent behaviors.

For the purposes of this book, the emphasis is on providing developmental information *and* behavior guidance strategies to support parents. For many, figuring out how to respond to behaviors we want to discourage is one of the greatest challenges of parenting. It asks us to do the emotional work of discovering and deciding (and rediscovering and redeciding) how we balance the warmth of our parenting with the firm side of our parenting.

This work is particularly challenging within the cultural confusion about the concepts of love and discipline. Specifically, the assumption that love always feels comfortable and conflict-free, while discipline equals punishment, pain, and fighting. It is often the case that we are at our most loving when we face the discomfort of being a parental leader.

When content is offered about child development, it is intended to provide a context for children's behavior so that parents can understand a little more fully when it is important to emphasize comfort and support vs. behavior guidance.

For example, a usually easygoing child who becomes unable to play safely with his sibling will need specific intervention to keep everyone safe. That intervention will look very different if Mom thinks that the irritability is based on being overly tired or hungry rather than a deliberate attempt to hurt. (See *Discipline Discussion, page 67.*) Content about behavior guidance is intended to help a parent recognize that the goal of discipline is not to cause physical or emotional pain, but to teach, so that ultimately the child will move from the external discipline of the parent or teacher to internal self-control and self-management as they mature.

Research indicates that children who are raised within the context of a Democratic/Authoritative parenting style are secure, have high self-esteem, demonstrate self-regulation and respect for others, and develop emotional resiliency.

TEMPERAMENT MATTERS

Temperament—yours and your child's—plays an important role in the parent-child relationship and in the support and guidance patterns that develop.

Differences, or even similarities, in temperament may help explain why some days just do not go well.

Opposites do not always attract, and may instead be a source of misunderstandings. An outgoing dad may be surprised at what overwhelms or upsets a child with a more introverted disposition. A "low sensitivity" parent may be impatient with a "high sensitivity" child who is bothered by the crease in his sock and can't do anything else until it is fixed.

At the same time, like temperaments come with their own challenges. For instance, parents might not find it easy to help their children through situations that they themselves still find challenging. For example, Mom, having internalized a sense of "being a disappointment" by being labeled "shy" as a child, may add feelings of powerlessness when hearing the same label applied to her preschooler. (See *Labels Impact Life*, page 131.)

Nine Traits of Temperament

A person will have varying levels and combinations of these traits.

- Activity
- Adaptability
- Rhythmicity or Regularity
- Sensitivity
- Distractibility
- Persistence
- Intensity
- Mood
- High Approach/More Cautious (Informally-Extroverted/Introverted)

(Source, Dr. S. Chess & Dr. A. Thomas)

As these examples show, it's important to understand your own temperament, your child's, as well as the temperaments of those central to your family life. It is also important to know in your heart that no temperament is superior or inferior.

SUPPORTING YOUR OWN TEMPERAMENT AND THAT OF YOUR CO-PARENT

Becoming aware of temperament will help you help your child, but don't forget to use it to help yourself and your primary adult relationship.

- Are you or your child more cautious in temperament? Then arrive at the playdate early so that you can enter into a smaller more manageable group; or make it a point to organize one-on-one playdates.

  - If you're paired with someone who loves novelty, it is OK to give yourself a few extra minutes to decide how to approach newness in increments that make it enjoyable for you too.

- Do you need more social stimulation than your child? Then absolutely make sure you set up adult time to be with your own friends and be as social and gregarious as you want to be. This is not an indulgence. It is necessary for you.

  - For co-parents, even the most reflective stay-at-home parent may need the opportunity to spend time with other adults to recharge after a day of preschool challenges.

  - For someone who has spent the day dealing with the social demands of employment, going out again may feel like overwhelm. For this parent, honoring temperament may mean a much-needed quiet time after children are in bed.

- Are you highly active? Then you will need to arrange with family or friends for "run time" if you've been trapped indoors for days with a child who has been ill.

- Are you a person of regular hours? Then you will need to create a pattern for mealtimes, and active and quiet times during the day to moderate your stress. If your patterns are disrupted significantly by children's needs, ask for the support you need to help put your body back into routine.

Remember, our children learn most from what we do. If you want your child to grow up to value herself and her own needs, you need to value yours, too. **Becoming a parent never means you stop being you.**

THE TEMPERAMENT TOOL

This exercise is one way to understand temperament. It is not meant to categorize anyone. It is a tool that may aid your exploration toward a better understanding of yourself, those you love, and the relationships between you and your loved ones.

In each box, mark the point along the continuum that best represents your child's expression of that particular trait. (If you are doing more than one child, you may find it helpful to use different colors to identify each person.) Do the same for yourself. As you do this exercise, don't think too hard: Trust your gut. You very likely have a strong intuitive understanding. For instance, before the child speaks her first word, a mom may hear herself reassuring well-intended relatives that her child enjoys a slower pace when meeting new people. Another parent may have learned that her child is so anxious to engage with a new activity she can hardly get the coat off fast enough.

As you do this exercise, also consider the age and development of your child. For example, most preschool children are physically active. How much your child exhausts you is probably not the best measure of his activity level. Consider instead his level of activity compared to his peers. Keep in mind that each point along the continuum represents a normal range of behavior. This means that whether high- or low-active, whether predictable or unpredictable, no expression of any trait is more "normal" than another.

Once you have completed each box for your child and then for yourself, you will have a good picture of your child's temperament and your own.

Next, ask yourself who else is important to your family or to your child. It might be a spouse or co-parent, a sibling, a grandparent, nanny or other caregiver. You'll see there is a third line in each box. Use this to add information about the other adult or offer it to them for their input. You may find that there is slight variation in where they place the child on the continuum. If their placement differs significantly from your scale, it is likely that the behaviors you see are something other than temperament.

Importantly, you have an easy-to-read visual representation of the ways in which you and your child are similar in temperament and the ways in which you are different. This may create an opportunity for adults to talk about child behaviors and better match behavior guidance strategies to temperament when support is needed.

ACTIVITY LEVEL

	High Activity					Low Activity				
MY CHILD	·	·	·	·	·	·	·	·	·	·
ME	·	·	·	·	·	·	·	·	·	·
_____	·	·	·	·	·	·	·	·	·	·

REGULARITY

	Predictable					Unpredictable				
MY CHILD	·	·	·	·	·	·	·	·	·	·
ME	·	·	·	·	·	·	·	·	·	·
_____	·	·	·	·	·	·	·	·	·	·

APPROACH/WITHDRAWAL

	Joins Easily					Observes Before Joining				
MY CHILD	·	·	·	·	·	·	·	·	·	·
ME	·	·	·	·	·	·	·	·	·	·
_____	·	·	·	·	·	·	·	·	·	·

ADAPTABILITY

	Accepts Change Easily	Resists Change
MY CHILD	· · · · ·	· · · · ·
ME	· · · · ·	· · · · ·
_____	· · · · ·	· · · · ·

MOOD

	Pleasant	Negative
MY CHILD	· · · · ·	· · · · ·
ME	· · · · ·	· · · · ·
_____	· · · · ·	· · · · ·

DISTRACTIBILITY

	High	Low
MY CHILD	· · · · ·	· · · · ·
ME	· · · · ·	· · · · ·
_____	· · · · ·	· · · · ·

SENSITIVITY

	High Reaction					Low Reaction				
MY CHILD	·	·	·	·	·	·	·	·	·	·
ME	·	·	·	·	·	·	·	·	·	·
_____	·	·	·	·	·	·	·	·	·	·

PERSISTENCE

	Persistent					Changeable				
MY CHILD	·	·	·	·	·	·	·	·	·	·
ME	·	·	·	·	·	·	·	·	·	·
_____	·	·	·	·	·	·	·	·	·	·

INTENSITY

	Strong					Subdued				
MY CHILD	·	·	·	·	·	·	·	·	·	·
ME	·	·	·	·	·	·	·	·	·	·
_____	·	·	·	·	·	·	·	·	·	·

TEMPERAMENT AND PARENTING

When you understand temperament, you are more equipped to guide and support your child. For instance:

When you know you have a high-activity child, you know that planning for a long car ride means also planning for stops along the way. Those stops may include getting out a soccer ball and spending five to ten minutes running at top speed before racing back to the car seat.

If you know you have a child who has a regular scheduled body clock, making travel plans that allow the child to eat and sleep at times that reflect that clock will make life easier for everyone.

Meanwhile, if you have a highly adaptable child, a day's disruption during travel may not particularly impact the quality of the day for either parent or child.

Understanding temperament can diffuse blame and judgment and help you **Know** and **Accept** your child as the whole, unique person he is.

A low-active mom with a high-active child might worry that her child is wild, out of control. "He is driving me crazy," she might say (and feel). Driven by her own need for calm, she may respond by trying to forcibly contain his energy. **Because we have a strong tendency to see our norm as the norm, Mom may believe that there is something wrong with her child.**

For this mom, it will be important to watch her child's activity schedule as much as the meal and snack schedule. Planning for intense physical activity by adjusting the family's space so that there is a safe place, and defining an appropriate time to be "really busy," will take some of the pressure off Mom.

Further, watching high-active children may give clues to how much is enough and how much is too much activity. When there has not been sufficient opportunity to slow down for short rests or food breaks, some high-activity children seem to continue a spiral of action that limits their overall ability to slow down when needed.

When the mom in the example understands temperament, she can make environmental adjustments so that the expression of his high-active temperament is better supported, and though Mom will very likely still be challenged by the differences in temperament, the challenge is now emptied of labels and language of blame or assumed intent to drive someone crazy.

Never is temperament more important than in finding the right learning environments for preschool children. Obviously, early learners need environments that support their expanding cognitive skills. However, the overall tone and emotional climate will be impacted for both children and teachers by the combination of their unique temperaments.

For early learners, having teachers/leaders who understand and are able to adapt to varying temperaments in a classroom will help children experience organized learning environments as safe, supportive, and fun. Many parents will find discussions with other parents and making classroom observations a valuable investment of time prior to enrollment. (See *The Preschool Decision,* page 135.)

Of course, Mom will still worry about her child. If not now, there will be something in the future. Parents worry. And that worry should be acknowledged for the resource that it is. But it is a much better resource—and, for the parent, a much healthier resource—when it has an informed base of knowledge to check with. Temperament is an important piece of this knowledge base, as are child development and information about age-appropriate expectations.

WHAT YOU NEED TO KNOW ABOUT TEMPERAMENT

We are, as current thinking holds, born with it.

No temperament is better than any other. Each has its strengths and challenges.

Temperament is resistant to change, but while a more introverted (more cautious) person may never become an extrovert, she can learn to comfortably do, and excel at "extroverted" things such as leading and speaking to large groups.

Temperament is different from age-appropriate behavior. Most preschool children need to be active; this does not necessarily mean they have a high-activity temperament.

Parents, family dynamics, and environment can influence how a child expresses his temperament.

Temperament traits are not either-or; each trait lies along a spectrum.

DISCIPLINE DISCUSSION

Often people equate "discipline" with "punishment" because historically, discipline was synonymous with causing physical or emotional pain. Authoritative/ Democratic parenting (see *Parenting Styles,* page 55) requires that adults shift their focus to teaching. At its core, discipline within the family teaches children that:

- They may not hurt themselves.

- They may not hurt others.

- They may not hurt or damage what the family values.

Ideally, discipline balances love and care with guidance and support. It helps children to develop the skills they will need on their journey to becoming competent adults. To do this well, parents need a variety of skills as well as deep knowledge of their children. Discipline can feel complicated and challenging in part because so many elements are in flux—children keep growing and changing; parents are growing and changing; jobs and neighborhoods are changing.

Parents cannot change their child's traits or their own family history. However, parents can learn to be aware of issues from their own childhood that may impact their comfort and skill in parenting children. They can also learn a variety of skills to best fit their children's temperaments and developmental stages.

The goal of parental discipline is to establish the framework for what will eventually become self-management and self-discipline. Guidance tools and strategies in this book reflect the changes in children as they develop.

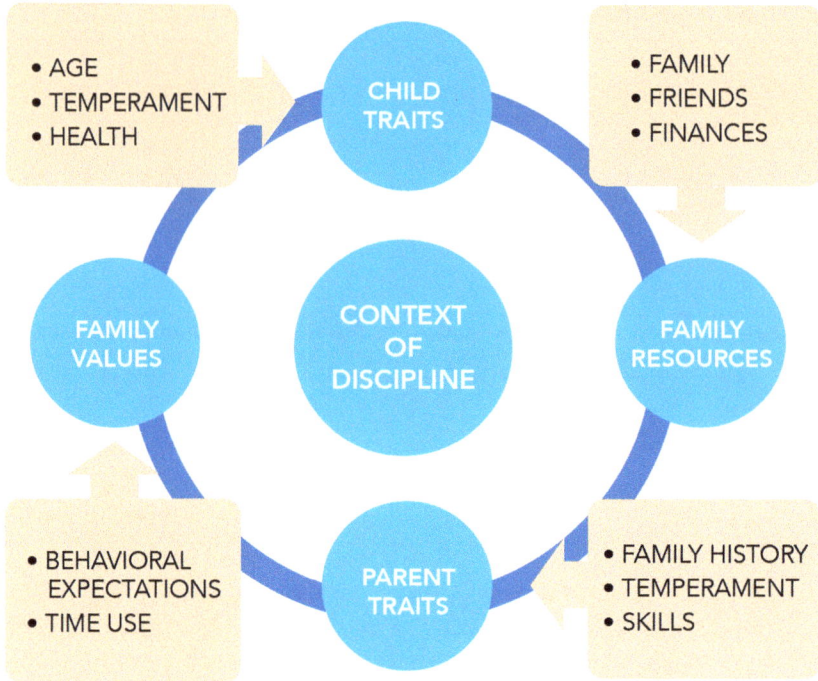

- AGE
- TEMPERAMENT
- HEALTH

CHILD TRAITS

- FAMILY
- FRIENDS
- FINANCES

FAMILY VALUES

CONTEXT OF DISCIPLINE

FAMILY RESOURCES

- BEHAVIORAL EXPECTATIONS
- TIME USE

PARENT TRAITS

- FAMILY HISTORY
- TEMPERAMENT
- SKILLS

DISCIPLINE BEGINS WITH THE ABCS

A is for Attachment

When children understand that parents and adults are offering guidance from a framework of care, they respond faster to behavioral guidance strategies. Children's early attachments are anchored in consistent physical care and the balance of calming and stimulating interactions from the caregivers.

B is for the Brain

Brain organization begins at the start of attachment. Infants and caregivers begin a reciprocal relationship that encourages co-regulation. Soon, children begin to demonstrate an understanding of cause and effect, after which they develop the basis for language and impulse control.

C is for Consistency

Consistency includes creating rituals and routines that support the daily flow of activities so that children can begin to trust their environment. Further, consistency in who is caring for the child provides the child with the opportunity to sustain early attachments and then, later, to expand the circle of trusted caregivers to involve extended family or friends. Finally, consistent follow-through with guidance strategies clarifies for children the nature of expectations, and allows them to more quickly internalize the seeds of self-discipline.

Discipline has a basic skill set. When and how the skills are implemented depends on the parent's interpretation of the social context, as well as parent and child temperament. For example, mealtime at home is a very different social context than mealtime at a restaurant. When a parent interprets all the elements of the context and responds within the basic discipline skill set, they often do very good parenting that looks different from the very good parenting of their friends and neighbors. The "interpretation factor" is reflected in how a parent reacts to advice they read in a book or hear from a well-intended friend. It may be absolutely true that the advice would never work for you because the author or friend has not allowed for the context nor the temperaments involved.

The Discipline Basics

- Environmental Management
- Redirection
- Time Out
- Time In
- Natural Consequences
- Logical Consequences
- Interpretation

THE DISCIPLINE BASICS

Environmental Management

This typically involves placing things out of reach or limiting their use. This is most often done to ensure safety, and to prevent or minimize child behavior that would otherwise demand constant/intense supervision. It is a common and particularly useful tool that we use with younger children, but it still works for older kids. Chaperones at a school dance provide environmental management, as does a lock on a liquor cabinet. It works for adults, too. After all, it is easier to resist cookies when they are put away in the cupboard than when they are sitting out on the counter in a cookie jar.

This powerful discipline strategy fails, however, when adults **ignore or do not plan for the environment, or forget that adults are the most powerful element in any environment!** Ignoring or not planning in advance for environmental differences when going to a friend's home may mean the difference between spending every minute watching children vs. having an enjoyable visit with other adults. Choosing the right sports team coach increases the opportunity for a safe, happy learning experience for children. Allowing children to go to homes that reflect our family values reinforces the model of family and interactions being taught at home.

Redirection

For young children, this involves physically redirecting attention, such as offering an engaging toy to redirect from an inappropriate one. For preschool and older children, we involve them in the redirection. (*"Looks like that game is scary for your younger sister. What else could you choose to do?"*)

Time In

This is about making amends, noticing others, and noticing how actions affect them. It is particularly appropriate when there was not negative intent on the part of the child, but it can also be used in other contexts. So, if toddler Jimmy, without any intent to harm, bumps too hard against toddler Luke, you could help make the connection for Jimmy ("Look at Luke's sad face, you bumped him too hard"), and engage in atoning ("I wonder how we can help Luke"). Jimmy might just watch as you model atonement, he might assist you as you follow through ("Let's go get him a glass of water"), or have his own idea, perhaps offering a toy or a kiss. Just be sure Jimmy's offer respects Luke's needs.

When Jimmy is ten and says he is going to Luke's house but instead ends up at Sam's, connect his actions to your worry, and engage Jimmy so that he reflects on his action and possible ways to rebuild your trust. Time in can be used with logical consequences. In this case, restricting independence, i.e., "Next time I will walk with you to Luke's house."

Time in is less effective in supporting siblings and peers in resolving difficulties when adults distract children from their work by demanding an apology, defining what will make it better, or doing too much thinking *for* the children. Below are a few phrases parents might use that could have unintended consequences.

- **"Say you're sorry."** Yes, as part of good manners it is important to teach children to apologize. For apologies to have meaning, however, they need to reflect an awareness of harm to the other as well as a sense of personal responsibility, which often doesn't develop until middle elementary age. A simple phrase such as, "When people do things that hurt others they say they are sorry. You'll learn how to do this," could help clarify meaning for the child.

- **"She needs a kiss from you."** When an outsider, even a well-intentioned parent, states what is required to make something better without first consulting the injured person, he or she risks creating a context in which the injured person may have boundaries violated.

- **"Give her the toy; she's littler than you."** Parents often wish for quick solutions to children's issues. When we attempt shortcuts, such as in this example, we risk jeopardizing future sibling relationships. Further, we may limit younger children from developing respect for personal boundaries or invite younger children to stay immature in their negotiating skills.

Time Out

The key features of time out are separation and non-engagement. The rule is generally one minute of time out per age of child. This consequence is best reserved for the most troublesome behaviors, typically those that harm others. When toddler Jimmy intentionally knocks Luke over, remove Jimmy, be brief in your explanation of why ("No pushing and hurting others"), and do not engage with Jimmy for two minutes. When it's done, it's done, and Jimmy can go back to playing. Although it will not help to ask a toddler with little or no impulse control to problem-solve, a preschool child can be reminded that it is important for his brain/head to help his muscles remember to be safe with his friends.

At about age seven, we ask children to use the time out to reflect on their choices. Time out should support self-reflection of behavior and planning for new behavior. The minutes still match the age. After the time out is complete, briefly engage ("What can you do differently now?").

Time out is often the least understood guidance strategy, in part because it is one strategy with two different meanings based on the child's developmental stage. For a toddler, the meaning of time out is a behavioral training connecting cause and effect, where the cause is the misbehavior and the effect is the consequence—time out. For older children, its intent is to create reflective time for acknowledging behavior and planning to do better.

Time out fails when adults pay too much attention to a child who is supposed to be in time out, or they allow themselves to be sidetracked by non-related behavior.

For example, holding a resistant child in a "time out chair" is actually giving the child undivided focus and attention, rather than non-engagement. Focusing on the back talk of a child whose body is actually moving to comply may divert both parent and child from the initial issue. (This does not mean that back talk is acceptable. It does mean that it can be addressed at another time and not used as a tool to sidetrack a parent.)

Natural Consequences

Let children (safely) experience the results of their actions. For example, if outside time will be brief, when children resist mittens, let them have the experience of cold hands. When your eight-year-old forgets her lunch *again*, resist the urge to run it to school. Remember that children often find a way to problem-solve, and experiencing and learning about natural consequences at age eight is important preparation for teenage years, when natural consequences can be something much more dangerous than a missed lunch.

Using Natural Consequences as a Discipline Strategy Requires:

- An understanding of the child's development
- A context in which no significant or long-term harm can come to the child

Natural Consequences Cannot Be Used When:

- The situation is too dangerous (we **never** allow frostbite to be a natural consequence)
- The natural consequence is too distant for the child to make the connection (lack of brushing and the cavity, for instance, are too distant)

- The natural consequence is too abstract for the child to comprehend ("How can I trust you now?" is too abstract for children until middle elementary)

Natural consequences fail as teaching tools when adults forget to describe the choice the child made, forget to verbalize the outcome of the child's choice, or do not allow the choice or the consequence to occur.

For example, fighting to put a child's hands in mittens does not allow a choice. (Again, this can only be a choice for a brief exposure to severe weather so that no long-term skin damage could occur.) Rushing a lunch to a child who left it at home does not allow a natural learning experience. (Many children increase their problem-solving skills by negotiating for a lunch with friends and others.) Writing an excuse note for school for a preteen who chose to stay up too late does not support developing personal responsibility, nor does it allow the social consequence of dealing with classroom expectations.

Logical Consequences

Like natural consequences, logical consequences require an understanding of the child's development; a context that does not cause long-term harm; and the opportunity for the child to not only choose, but to experience the results of their choices/actions. The long-term benefits of logical consequences are that children become aware of the impact of their behavior on themselves and others.

There are several challenges for parents using logical consequences as teaching tools. The first is that the consequence must be related to the event and so clearly tied to the outcome of the choice that it is logical to the child. For instance, a logical consequence for a demand such as, "Get me a snack," is to give no snack until the request is made more respectfully. It is never a bad guidance strategy to remind a child how to be successful. The logical consequence for the older child who said she would do her chores, but by bedtime has not, can be to set a specific time for chores. The consequence of her misuse of time is that she now has less control over her time.

The underlying goal of a logical consequence is to help children think about their choices at the time they make the choice. Whenever possible, ask children (age three and above) what they think the consequence might be.

Logical Consequences Require:

- An understanding of the child's development—can the child understand choice, and does he have some impulse control?

To Be Effective, Logical Consequences Must:

- Be related to the event

- Be clear

- Allow choice

- Follow directly after the event

Because the sense of time is abstract and can be challenging for children for several years, logical connections often need to be repeated in matter-of-fact tones. "Remember: you chose to eat a cookie for dessert; that means it isn't time for ice cream tonight." For an elementary child, "Remember: you chose to do homework right after supper so that you could play outside; that means homework comes before TV tonight."

To avoid offering choices that invite power struggles or sound like threats ("If you don't... I won't let you..."), it often helps to:

FRAME THE CHOICE AS AN EITHER-OR

Either you may _____, or you may _____. You decide.

FRAME THE CHOICE AS A WHEN-THEN

When you _____, then you may _____.

When children are age three or older, engage them in the process by asking what they think the logical consequence should be. For example, when boys forget to put their bikes in the garage, what should happen?

Logical consequences are less effective discipline teaching tools when they are unclear and the "logic" is not linked in the child's mind. Parents need to ask themselves: can the child find the logical link between these common parent reactions and the children's behavior? (Remember that discipline is teaching.)

- Siblings fighting—no TV?

- A low grade in a class—no phone use?

- Room not cleaned—grounded for a week?

Further, parents are challenged to watch themselves in threatening consequences and then withdrawing them or forgetting to follow through with them. Emotionally, for a loving parent, it can be very difficult to allow a child to make a choice knowing that, as part of the initial learning process, the child is very likely to experience an outcome or consequence that includes disappointment or sadness later.

Perhaps you have also encountered this example in a grocery store? You overhear a parent say, "If you don't walk with me, you have to ride in the cart." The child wanders and is put in the cart, but begins to fuss, so the parent withdraws the consequence and gives another chance. As the observer, would you guess that the child is learning: "If I wander I have to be in the cart"? Or is it more likely the child is learning: "If I fuss in public I won't have to ride in the cart"?

Finally, logical consequences fail as a discipline-teaching strategy when parents give in to the great temptation of saying, "I told you so…" rather than allowing the circumstance to be a teaching event.

The parent may want to say, "I told you your hands would be cold if you didn't put on your mittens," but reporting the logical consequence would be saying instead, "Cold fingers aren't fun. Mittens are good protectors to keep fingers warm." Or, rather than saying, "I told you that you wouldn't like doing homework after supper," the parent reporting the logical consequence could say, "It's hard to know how disappointed you can be to miss watching TV after supper."

"I told you so" comments build resentment against the speaker, rather than allowing the consequence to teach.

Interpretation

Interpretation is dependent on awareness—body and spirit; emotional and physical; internal and external; self and other. Although this may sound esoteric, it is more than a mystical trait only a few have or can develop. Parental awareness is supported by knowing about child development. It may be common knowledge that children have temper tantrums, and that often a strategy of ignoring them during the tantrum is a way to diminish the number and intensity of tantrums. It is interpretation and parental awareness that manages a tantrum by including the context of a child who is over tired from a trip to the zoo, and instead of ignoring offers support and a drink of water. Interpretation and parental awareness may even be used to "head it off at the pass" by leaving the zoo before the child has reached the limit of their physical and emotional reserves.

Interpretation is more difficult or distorted when adults do not manage the baggage from their own history, when they ignore temperament or developmental challenges in the environment. In particular, parents who have learned to be afraid of their feelings or the feelings of others can experience an internal struggle to figure out when to use empathy to support children vs. one of the other discipline strategies.

WE MIGHT HAVE A VACUUM, BUT WE DON'T LIVE IN ONE

Families exist within a wider community and an even wider society. In the past, parenting advice and opinions were things individual parents would seek out for themselves—the province of books and private conversations. Today, parenting is a national conversation. On the one hand, it's about time! The art of parenting is fascinating and wonderfully complex. Nurturing the next generation couldn't be a more essential topic for society as a whole. Yet, this new attention can also bring unwanted pressure, stress, and influence on those actually engaged in the complicated business of childrearing. (See *Peers and Peer Pressure*, page 123.) The talk is loudest around the sensational and the controversial, such as the practice of labeling mothers as "Tiger," "Free-Range" or "Calorie-Restricting" Mom. And, unfortunately, all this controversy can seep into our life with our children—even without us knowing it.

- Your child takes a spill at the mall and you hold yourself back from giving comfort, lest eyes around you scream: "Helicopter parent!"

- Your family's personal decision about piano lessons for your oldest is suddenly muddied by other voices in your head—"Don't! You're over-scheduling her." Or, "Do it, she needs the discipline or she'll become one of those *entitled* kids."

- A dustup on the playground gets out of hand and your child asks for help. Your instincts tell you that this spat needs a bit of guidance, but out of the ether words form in your head: "These kids have got to learn to fight their own battles." So instead you say, "Figure it out."

The good news is, unlike the context of the child's temperament and developmental stage, we do have control over outside influence, but only if we take a moment to recognize it and evaluate it against our own beliefs and traditions. To stop and find that moment can feel like a luxury. Likewise, it may not be easy to find time to think about discipline—what you want it to be and what you want it to feel like for your child or children—and then find even more time to discuss it with any parenting partners. But the payoff in time, ease, mental energy, and family well-being is totally worth it.

RULES ABOUT RULES

When thinking about the rules of the family, it is often helpful to have a clear understanding of the potential pitfalls that accompany the establishment and implementation of family rules. The following questions may help you bring clarity to the process.

ARE YOUR RULES WELL DEFINED OR UNCLEAR?

Children do better when rules are well defined and, as much as possible, stated in terms of concrete behaviors and outcomes. Remember that the younger the child is, the more concrete the rule needs to be. For example, rather than saying, "Pick up your toys," it is often more helpful to preschoolers if they are presented with a reminder of a fact, such as, "The cars and trucks go in the box." Keeping the rule concrete and specific is appropriate to their developmental understanding at this stage. When children are older and the pattern well established, the larger category of "toys" and where things belong will be better integrated. For children of all ages, when the rule is perceived as unclear, children will remain dependent on the adult to correct and monitor the outcome until the nature of the rule becomes clear.

ARE YOUR RULES REASONABLE OR UNREASONABLE?

Every parent intends to be reasonable. Despite this good intention, a rule becomes unreasonable when:

The child is unable to do the behavior.

"Clean up your room" is a requirement that is not only unclear (based on the number of various pieces that make up a "room" and what "clean" looks like), but the developmental demand to stay focused on a large task with multiple components can be well beyond the level of maturity for most early elementary children. Keeping company, coaching the child through the skills needed, and providing visual charts are often helpful as children grow into learning to care for their environment.

There is no necessity to require the behavior.

"Stay in your bed" may seem perfectly reasonable to a parent who envisions his or her child safe and snug while sleeping. However, children do not seem to need particularly soft surfaces for sleep. Does it really matter if the child sleeps on the floor? What does matter is that the child's sleep space be safe. This will mean that the parent must ensure that the whole room is a safe sleep environment. Experienced parents have moved dressers away from windows and securely anchored them to the wall or moved them into closets to lessen climbing hazards. They have removed lamps and electrical hazards that could create risk, gated bedroom doorways, and provided other environmental adaptations to protect their young children from risk.

The rule attempts to control or eliminate behavior that is normal and desirable.

"Stop throwing, running, climbing, talking…!" As you can see, these are all healthy, normal behaviors that we hope to see in children when it is appropriate. They are not activities that are in themselves undesirable, but perhaps become undesirable if they are happening with the wrong object, in the wrong place, or at the wrong time for the adult. For the preschooler, running is simply what you do to get somewhere quickly. The goal of the parent is to guide the child into when and where it is OK to run. In this case, walking safely with Mom in the parking lot is a rule that will need to be reinforced often. Children may need to be reminded that running to the playground is all right *as soon as their feet are on the grass*. This is true for many other child behaviors.

The rule requires more to enforce than you, the parent, have time to maintain.

"Stay in your bed" may not only be unnecessary, it may also demand more energy and patience than a parent has at the end of a long day. No loving but exhausted parent wants the bedtime ritual to include carrying a child back to his bed every two minutes for an hour!

ARE YOUR RULES ENFORCEABLE OR UNENFORCEABLE?

When a rule is made, it is important to enforce it every time until the new behavior is learned, AND to ignore any behaviors not covered by the rule. For example, establishing a rule about when to turn off the television may result in a child's attempt to influence that decision through tears, pouting, or displays of temper. Even when the parent has been respectful in informing the child about the rule before the event, and reminding her about the rule while turning the TV off, in the moment, children may express their disappointment with more intensity than most adults would exhibit. However, when parents do not enforce the rule in an attempt to avoid the child's tears, pouting, or temper, the rule becomes unenforceable.

ARE YOUR RULES NEGOTIABLE OR NON-NEGOTIABLE?

There are times when rules must be non-negotiable:

Safety and Health

"You can hold my hand or ride in the cart" may feel like negotiation, however, the underlying non-negotiable message is, "I will keep you safe."

"You can have applesauce or juice after you take your antibiotic," also allows for some feeling of negotiation, but in the end it's non-negotiable that "Mom will be sure you take your medicine."

Respect for Self and Supporting Autonomy

"When you pass gas your body is saying *I have to go potty*. Do you want Momma or Daddy to keep you company?" is a way to convey the message: "Care for your body/self is an important job for you to do. We will help you."

Respect for Others

"I see your sister wasn't using her crayons when you wanted them. Did you ask her if it was a time when you could use them?" is a way of reminding your child of the rule to respect others' property and boundaries by first asking for permission from the owner.

Family Values

"Our family likes books; we'll help your little sister learn which books are hers so yours are not torn," showcases the value the family places on books and reading and establishes a rule that supports that value.

When children have integrated the basic elements of life's non-negotiable rules, *negotiable rules allow for practice making choices and exploring personal power.* The opportunity for this kind of practice contributes to the development of personal responsibility and expressions of preferences. For example, the non-negotiable bedtime may be preceded by a bedtime ritual that allows the child to choose which two books are read. Snack time may allow the child to choose which of two fruits will be eaten. As some of the examples above indicate, negotiable elements may be incorporated into non-negotiable structures. But for now, your preschool child is dependent on you to determine when tasks and time are non-negotiable.

WHO'S IN CHARGE? POWER STRUGGLES

It is both humbling and frightening when we feel responsible but don't actually have the power to control every what, when, where, and how that we encounter as a parent. Particularly vexing are the Big Three: eating, sleeping, and toileting. When an infant struggles with feeding, it can invite feelings of failure on the part of a new mother. When a toddler struggles with the transition from three naps to two, or two naps to one, outings and errands become even more unpredictable. But, as challenging as those days once were, they can seem easy in comparison to the active resistance of a preschool child.

So…do the battles never end? Well, to be honest, no, they don't. And, honestly, you don't want them to end. Power struggles are part of figuring out who you are in the world and who you are in relationship to others. Preschool children, especially, need to explore power. And, as parents of preschoolers, we are called on to consider our own understanding of power.

We all need power over our own bodies—physical power to go and do, and thereby strengthen, grow, and learn. We need verbal power to express our boundaries as well as our preferences. We need power in relationships with others to manage those times when we are called to lead, follow, or collaborate. We see then how power is used to claim a variety of roles through which we express the multiple facets that make us a complex whole. Adults have had years to both explore and integrate a variety of expressions of power, but it's all new to the preschooler. As their social world grows, so do arenas in which to explore and express power. However, for most, the immediate family will be the dominant space in which day-to-day exploration and practice of power takes place.

SEPARATE AND *ATTACHED*

It's important to recognize that it is not just the preschooler, but also the parent who is now exploring an expanded definition of personal boundaries. The infant has no sense of boundaries, feeling, instead, *Mom is an extension of me*. The toddler has a beginning sense of boundaries. (Remember the shouts of "Mine!") But the mind and spirit of a preschooler are mature enough to recognize the separateness of caregiver from child—to understand, *Mom is separate from me.*

But separateness is different from detachment. Well-loved preschool children are attached to those who are their caregivers, and from that attachment are able to form more attachments of varying degrees. Yes, they will—we hope—love their preschool teacher, but it will be nothing like the love they have for Mom and Dad.

Remembering this developing separateness can help bring clarity about where to place parental energy, spirit, and intellect. Take, for example, the so-called "picky" eater. This is when it is helpful to recognize the separate responsibilities of the adult and the child. The adult provides the food. The child decides how much of it to eat. The adult makes choices related to texture, taste, nutrition, presentation, etc., but ultimately it is the child's job to decide how much food to put into her mouth and stomach. A mother who is confused about this boundary may find herself imposing artificial rules on eating. Some of which can backfire in the long term. For example, the statement, "*No dessert unless you eat your peas,*" can feed into the belief that dessert is to be valued over other foods.

NO ONE WINS POWER STRUGGLES OVER EATING, SLEEPING, OR TOILETING

Although it is possible to physically overpower a child enough to put a winter coat on a resistant body, there's no forcing eating, sleeping, and toileting. The role of the adult is to set the environment, to coach and to guide a child to personal success. This means placing parental energy, spirit, and intellect into observing children's responses, reflecting on our language and our leadership behavior, and being attentive to our own feelings about the area of concern.

"Am I a good mom if my child doesn't eat what I put in front of her?"

You may remember the baby scale, the close attention to every ounce of an infant's weight gain, and also to every ounce of milk or formula consumed. All this (necessary) attention on growth and feeding at the infant stage can spill over, however, so that food intake, inadvertently and perhaps unconsciously, becomes a measure to judge "good" or "bad" parenting.

This is when awareness of separateness and boundaries is particularly helpful. Instead of getting into a cycle of self-blame, we instead begin by understanding how much is enough. If a child has had three bites of meat, and an adult portion size is roughly the size of a standard deck of cards—three bites may be enough! Adults with a clean plate tradition who use a serving spoon to define the amount on the plate may only compound confusion about how much food a child really needs to eat at a meal. The human stomach is roughly about the size of the fist. So looking at your child's fist, it may be amazing that they eat as much as they do. And when on a growth spurt, there are times when it may seem there is no end to their interest in eating.

If, however, the child resists particular textures, parents may be called on to use intellect and creativity to offer quality food in a format the child can enjoy. One of the most common ways to include more vegetables is to puree them and put them in baked goods or spaghetti sauce. There are several cookbooks that provide engaging and fun recipes that can help take some of the struggle out of meals. Sharing food preparation places the child in the role of collaborator. Often children are less likely to resist something they had a hand in making.

Bedtime is primetime for a power struggle

When it comes to taking charge and expressing their separateness, children can be incredibly creative. One more drink of water, one more potty stop, one more story are all powerful ways to avoid the demand to sleep.

At naptime, rather than insist that a child nap, set the environment to have a regular afternoon rest time. Reassure the child that they do not need to sleep, but that everyone's body needs an afternoon rest time. Some children find it fun to know that there are whole countries that take an afternoon rest. They call it *siesta*. Others find it important to know the science of sleep. Young bodies grow when they sleep (hence, babies and teens need a lot of sleep!). So if it is a day when a child's body is ready to grow more than it can do during night sleep, then he will sleep during rest time. If not, it's okay for children to enjoy their quiet play time. During sleep we are also better able to move newly learned content into long-term memory. Every *body*, adult bodies included, heals and renews the immune systems during sleep. (For an expanded discussion of resistance at bedtime see *Sleep,* page 169.)

"No I won't and you can't make me!" is never truer than in toileting

There are so many variables involved in toileting resistance that when children have issues they may be related to things *other than exploring personal power.*

» Fears can get in the way and come from a variety of sources:

> *Imagination:* if you sat down on a potty chair and part of your body fell off, would you be afraid?

> *Pain:* having held a bowel movement too long may create an association of pain with toileting.

> *Sounds:* public restrooms are loud; conversely, home bathrooms may be too removed from the regular sounds of family activity so that children feel frightened by being alone.

> *Lack of control:* Auto-flush toilets have created a challenge for more than one child. High-pressure hand dryers can also be disturbing for some children.

> *Physical uncertainty:* Being perched on a too-large toilet also creates tension or fear, as well as the physical demand for balancing while trying to manage the task.

» Emotional ambivalence about being a "big kid" is a real challenge for children who may have younger siblings who receive undivided attention from caregivers around diapering.

» Internal struggles with developing executive function may be playing a role. Executive function helps us to do the things we don't want to, simply because they need to be done. As adults, we stop at red lights not because we want to, but because it needs to be done to keep others and ourselves safe. We have internalized values of personal and group safety and make decisions that inconvenience us in order to accommodate those values. Growing up is a physiological process of developing executive function. The immature brain, then, is more prone to focus on the short-term gain (ignoring internal cues and "holding it" so as not to interrupt play) and not the greater loss (disappointed caregivers and even more time lost to clean up).

For parents, getting out of a power struggle may be a struggle too. Here's what can help:

Be clear about your leadership role. We know that if we want polite children we need to model using good manners. However, you cannot always use rational discussion or coaxing to make another person want what you want them to want! Your desire for them to go to bed without a struggle, or to eat something you've prepared, is real and appropriate. However, spending a great deal of time telling them why they should want to eat that meal, or why they should want to go to bed is not only unsatisfying, it is often ineffective. Rather than getting caught up in justifying our leadership decisions, we can simply state the applicable rule: "Remember, eight o'clock is bedtime for four-year-olds." And we can certainly make it fun—asking with a smile, "Who in this house is four years old and wants to race Daddy to the bedroom to find pjs?"

Our young children are being who they are at their particular stage of development. Their feelings of "want" or "don't want" are untethered by understanding the benefits of sleep schedules and appropriate food choices. Our leadership role is often to create

The poet e e cummings can help us understand why, despite our sound arguments, we fail to gain collaboration from young children.[1]

Almost anybody can learn to think or believe, but not a single human being can be taught to feel. Why? Because whenever you think or believe or you know, you're a lot of other people: but the moment you feel, you're nobody-but-yourself.

[1]From "A Poet's Advice to Students," e e cummings's response to a letter from a high school editor; published in Ottawa Hills (Grand Rapids, Michigan) *High School Spectator*, October 26, 1955.

the context in which they will learn to make decisions for themselves when they have a more mature understanding of why a particular option may be better than another.

Remember that more or louder words are not the answer. Children can sound like short adults; however, they do not reason like adults. Words—even LOUD words—from a parent are not nearly as powerful as an inanimate object like a timer. Let the clock or timer "tell" the child when playtime is over or the TV must go off. This allows Mom or Dad to be on the child's side as she expresses disappointment that the "timer says we're done."

Describe, describe, describe the behavior and offer a choice for them to self-regulate. "I see a girl who's not remembering how to sit on the sofa. Is this a time you can sit, or do you need to find a jumping place?"

Remind them of the rule. "Remember, when we get out of the van, we hold hands in the parking lot because cars can't see you."

Ask them to remember the rule. "What's our rule about walking in the parking lot?"

Use imagination and humor, but never at their expense. A child resistant to getting dressed in the morning may be encouraged by a talking shirt sleeve. "Help me, help me! I need an arm! I'm too floppy to have fun today without an arm to help me!"

Play dumb. "Did we forget to tell you the rule about spitting? What a funny thing for a teacher to forget to tell her friends about how we do school here."

Engage them in problem-solving. "How do you think we should do it so everyone has a turn?"

The exploration of power will continue in many contexts. Children may try echoing words in a tone that parents find difficult. They may roll their eyes, or use verbal challenges or name calling, all of which may be normal but still represent unacceptable behavior. The use of consequences that are directly related to their choices is often the most powerful tool an adult can bring to guiding children as they continue to explore their power through words, tones, and non-verbal cues.

> Children live in the moment. When you see a preschool child break a rule, it is often more helpful to respond positively as though they do not "know the rule" or do not "remember the rule," rather than with a reprimand.

WHY DOES EVERYTHING ALWAYS HAVE TO BE AN ARGUMENT?

Remember **when you celebrated your little one's first words?** Well now that he or she is not so little, this wonderful tool of speech may evoke in you a much wider range of feelings. The power of speech enhances and supports development, and, as we know from every "*No!*" "*Why?!*" and "*I don't wanna!*" it can also invite extended conflict into relationships with peers, siblings, and parents.

PRESCHOOL BEGINNINGS

When preschool children begin to explore the nature of speech in relationships, they may attempt using it to gain power over peers or to push back on parental power. Telling a friend that he can't play, or beginning negotiation for one more story, one more drink of water, or one more potty stop before sleep are all familiar examples.

With Peers

This incredible tool of speech creates an opportunity to expand on "story" during play and **invites negotiation with peers about who is to play certain roles and how the "story" will continue.** (For example, creating the rule, "You have to drive the blue car over there to get the treasure.") If the play has been somewhat predefined by media characters the children already perceive as being either good or bad, or obvious leaders or followers, adults may overhear children actively resisting being cast into certain roles. Although preschool children are rarely able to express why, they are, at some level, aware of a trait or activity associated with a play character that they literally do not want to "try on." It may be because certain traits are incongruent with their beginning sense of self.

The child who persists in being "The Director" will **need help at times to create space for the others to negotiate a role** in the play. Children who express distress at being cast in a role may also **need support from an adult to have their preferences acknowledged by the others.** Whether the expanded negotiation results in entering the play or in a choice to join another activity, there is great value in knowing that one has been heard. It is **important that adults resist the temptation to label children** as bossy, uncooperative, or as crybabies.

Further, the expectation that others have a voice to be honored and that one cannot always be in charge helps lay a framework for later social interactions with peers. The current work with school bullies and bystanders seeks to reinforce these important messages for older children.

With Parents

When the tool of speech is used to explore or push back on parental leadership, it is important for adults to use those great gifts of routine and simple choices to support their children. If the routine is, for example, to always read two books, say a prayer, and then receive an extra special hug from Mom and Dad before lights out, then when the negotiation for more books begins the adult can:

- Remind the child of the routine,

- Reinforce the power of words—spoken and written—by writing down the requested book title so that it can be read first tomorrow night (or possibly read in the morning),

- Potentially affirm their interest in reading it themselves, and

- Model a calm trust that "this is the way the world works in this house."

Parents and other adult leaders play an important role in helping children internalize their understanding of the nature of rules. Children, for their part, will seek out and expand their interest in play that supports this huge life task. At or near age six, board games and entry sports that have clear rules become interesting. Moving from "picking up interesting stuff" toward organizing and categorizing collections reflects the brain's ability to bring order and "higher level" mental rules about things that belong together.

Older preschool children will have a period of "tattling," reporting when others are breaking the rules. Sometimes the motivation lies in experimentation with power to get another child in trouble. To lessen the likelihood that telling on others will become a tool to use against a sibling or another child, it is often best to simply reassure the teller that he or she is "remembering the rule," and that Mom/Dad will help the other child learn the rule, too. This affirms the child has it "right" without adding more pressure to the sibling/friend relationship.

Some families find that a weekly **"family meeting"** can be helpful. It's a time to discuss the week ahead, chore assignments, and to follow-up with last week's successes and challenges. More than just an organizational tool, the family meeting provides a formal structure in which children can understand this whole idea of rules, and the ways in which rules can be useful and relevant (instead of arbitrary). **Listening and valuing their input** often brings with it the advantage of better overall adult-child interactions, as well as better follow-through with chores and, often, more creativity in the way things get done.

WHINING

PHYSIOLOGY

Why is whining so irritating? Because it is linked to our survival. The grating complaint of a whine shares the pitches and tones of an infant's distressed cry, as well as the moans and groans of a person in pain. Adult ears are hardwired to respond to these pitches and tones. Whining is supposed to get under our skin. It is part of the built-in feedback loop that ensures our babies are warm and fed, and the hurt are helped.

Loving, supportive caregivers often find themselves particularly (dis)stressed by whining. A signal of distress in the very youngest of children usually signals the most basic of needs—food, protection, security, and comfort.

Whining will sometimes be the first clue that your child is sick or somehow distressed. Although we are expected to use words, we never outgrow our ability to whine. Children will naturally rely more on this biologically based call for help because it is so powerful as a communication tool.

But, just as a fever can be distressing to a child, so can the mild (to us) disappointment of not getting a cookie when he "really, really wants one!" Because learning how the world works—at home, at school, or in the store—is a major task for young children, the way parents respond to whining involves teaching.

In order to respond successfully, parents must become aware of their own autopilot responses, which may include all kinds of unintended reinforcements—gifting the child with additional attention, the desired cookie, or Momma's help.

Because the grating sound of a whine is so difficult to ignore, it can be an effective way to get attention. Whining becomes a problem when it is used not as a signal of true distress, but as a normal way to communicate. When your child whines, the first challenge is to discern whether it is signaling a problem that must be attended to. If, instead, the whine is an expression of inconvenience, impatience, or dissatisfaction, the challenge becomes **not** to respond to a request made with a whine. Then, teach and model for your child what kinds of sounds you will respond to (even if your response remains "no").

Whining:
What to do to stop the whine

FIRST Determine the Why of the Whine

NOT SURE?
1. Trust your gut
2. Err on the side of support and help

IF

the whine is rooted in a real and strong physical distress, such as exhaustion or the first stage of a cold, then:

SUPPORT AND HELP YOUR CHILD

Save the behavioral training for another time.

IF NOT

teach that whining is *not* an acceptable way to communicate:

DO NOT RESPOND TO THE WHINE

- Do not meet a request that is made with a whine.
- Pretend as if you cannot understand words that are spoken in a whine.

THE ART OF IGNORING

Though parents are often advised to *simply* "ignore the whine," ignoring is far from *simple*. To ignore does not mean to be silent, nor should it ever feel like a snub.

- Ignoring is not only about words. When your body stiffens, your shoulders tense, you quicken your pace, or furrow your brow, you are *not* ignoring; you are responding.

- Your silence won't help the child be successful. Though to get your message to your child, it's often helpful to direct your words to someone else, the thin air, or even the family pet.

Oooh! There's a sound that hurts my ears.

Spot, did you hear something? That sound was too whiny and squeaky for my ears to understand.

What is that *squeaky whiny* sound? Where did Owen's voice go? Is it hiding in the cupboard? In the refrigerator?

Silliness can be a great cure for a child's frustration, as well as your own. Pulling on your own reserves of humor can help you to teach with a light touch.

THEN show your child how to make a request you CAN respond to. The following tools [🔧] can help.

Remember: Behaviors tend to escalate before they change. Be persistent and patient.

USE WHEN-THEN TO TEACH WHAT SOUNDS ARE SUCCESSFUL

Avoiding the battleground language of "ifs" and "don'ts" (*if you don't stop, I'll...*), use "when-then" to matter-of-factly report what sound you CAN hear and CAN respond to.

Gram-meee, I want more pudding.

I cannot understand that *squeaky, whiny* sound.

When I hear Maya's regular voice **then** I can help Maya.

I DON'T WANNA!

WHINE AND CHEESE PARTY

HAVE A WHINING PARTY

Set a timer and have a short whining party. The whole family can join in. This will help your child understand what a whine sounds like and feels like. Also, on a day that seems full of whines, a whining party can provide a nice outlet. Often the energy will shift to laughter. In any case, if the party is set to a timer, everyone, especially the concrete thinking preschooler, will know it is time to stop.

USE YOUR OWN VOICE TO DEMONSTRATE THE SOUND THAT *DOESN'T* WORK AND THE SOUND THAT *DOES* WORK

Make your own voice whine as you describe the whiny sound you cannot respond to. Then bring your voice down to it's normal tone as you describe the sound you *will* respond to.

Remember, we do not *decide* to whine. Your child may not even be aware she is doing it. Demonstrating the sounds will help her become aware.

Even with highly-developed language and abstract thinking skills, adults find it hard to accurately describe the sound of a whine, yet we all know it when we hear it. Let your child hear it. As you wait, have your child demonstrate asking without the whine. This lets your child not only hear your difference, but to experience the feel of the sound from the inside as he makes his attempt to ask without the whine.

Mom!

VS.

Mom...

Whining is an all-ages behavior. Expect to reteach this lesson over and over again.

WHEN your child asks correctly be sure to respond
even if your answer is still no.

ACKNOWLEDGE THE ACCOMPLISHMENT

> You knew exactly how to ask mom.

Children love the feeling of accomplishment. Even if he does not get what he wants, he does get your attention and support for mastery of a skill.

HONOR THE THINKING AND NAME IT

> You are thinking it would be a good idea to have a cookie.

Putting words to his thought process supports language and problem-solving skills. It also supports his sense of self by confirming that he is a person who knows something about himself.

RESPOND HONESTLY

> This is a time when we don't have cookies. Remember, we have cookies after our sandwich.

A "No" delivered with empathy can lessen the frustration of being thwarted from what we want.

HELP PROBLEM-SOLVE

> You can have an apple! Come choose one. Watch me while I cut it up.

For example you can:

- Offer an acceptable alternative
- Make the temptation disappear
- Use distraction
- Give in imagination what you won't give in the present.
  What kind of cookie would you have if we had some in our house?

WHY THE LIES?

Lying is a normal part of child development. But does knowing this stop us from feeling uneasy or frustrated when our little ones pull out a whopper? No, or not much, and that's important. Feeling some discomfort is good. Understanding that it is common for children to lie makes it easier to respond without anger or shaming, while that feeling of discomfort reminds us to model honesty and to gently reinforce and teach the value of truth-telling.

TRUTH AND IMAGINATION

The made-up stuff we hear from our **preschoolers** is such a normal part of growing up that there is a term for the practice: *Primary Lying*. Little kids fib, they tell tall tales; in fact, some research suggests a correlation between lying and higher IQ.

In the young brain, fantasy and reality are easily meshed. We see this in the very common phenomenon of imaginary friends, which are created sometimes for companionship and play, but also sometimes as a scapegoat. It is easy for the young brain to slip from reality (*Mom wants me to brush my teeth but I didn't*) to the realm of wishing (*I want to make Mom happy*), so that the voice in the little one's head can easily move the desire (*I wish I did, I wish I did*) into a new reality (*I did. I did do it!*). And then you have a four-year-old utterly sincere in the conviction that she did indeed brush her teeth, even though she did not!

In general, **school-age children** are expected to be better able to distinguish fantasy and reality. They can also recognize the nature of honesty and are more aware that the act of lying is a conscious choice. But this is a gradual, ongoing process. We can expect children to begin to comprehend these concepts around **age five**. Most typically developing children will solidly get it by **age seven**, though some may take a little longer. If they continue to lie beyond age seven, it is more likely to disrupt the development of personal responsibility.

NOT ALL LIES ARE CREATED EQUAL

We use the tooth brushing example above for a reason: though lying may seem to be an effort to get out of doing something, quite often lying is based in the **desire to please**. From the child's immature perspective, by telling you what you want to hear she is pleasing you. She may even be confused when her fib elicits anger or disappointment from you.

There may even have been a time when you heard your child lie and actually felt proud. "Just what I wanted!" a child exclaims when she opens a gift she already has. This is called *Prosocial Lying*—an untruth meant to protect or benefit someone else, or what most of us call a "white lie."

Besides lying to please others, we can also lie to **make ourselves look good**, to **avoid punishment**, and—the biggie—to intentionally **cause harm**, or—another biggie—to lie for the **pleasure of lying**. Adults tend to see lying in terms of trust, and the lie, then, as some kind of fracture of the relationship. For young children, lying is instrumental and does not carry these same interpersonal implications.

> Remember that the motivation behind the lie is as important as the lie.

NURTURING HONESTY

To help children on their developmental journey we can:

- Support the child's ongoing effort to distinguish wish from reality. (How? See examples below.)

- Model honesty in our own behavior.

- Do our best not to allow the child to benefit from lying. (Be careful with this one so as not to unduly shame as you teach—see below.)

- Discuss the value of honesty and the concept of lying (when age-appropriate).

- Include age-appropriate stories on the subject in your bedtime ritual.

A Useful Tool. Until around age six or seven it is very difficult for a child to lie without turning herself in. When telling a lie, young children involuntarily smile and avert their eyes. The body's natural confessor can help parents identify lying and thus respond appropriately so that this common developmental behavior does not become habitual.

Parenting Pitfalls. Asking "Did you!?" in an accusing or threatening tone is likely to get one response: *precisely the one that children think we want to hear.* Asking "Why did you?" of a child who is too immature to reflect on personal behavior invites the child to create a story to answer the question. Asking when we already know the answer also may invite a variation of lying. *If we saw our child knock her glass over, there is no reason to ask, "Did you spill your milk?"*

Instead, by reporting what we saw—"*I see a girl who bumped her glass*"—then supporting the child to learn how to recover the event—"*Time to get the mop*"—we help children learn there is no reason to create a story (lie) about the event.

Prevention. Common sense suggests it, but research also supports it: in families that value and practice honesty there is reduced problematic lying in children.

> Part of our work as parents is being aware of how our responses to our children may unintentionally invite our children to lie.

RESPONDING TO LYING
(Sample Scenarios)

When There Is Evidence

The **four-year-old** in the tooth brushing example above still needs to brush her teeth. She also needs guidance that will support her growing understanding of the difference between what is true and what she wishes were true. Here is how the parent might respond:

Report the wish and report the evidence that suggests the wish is not reality.

The wish: "*You wish you had already brushed your teeth so you wouldn't have to stop playing to go brush.*"

The evidence: "*I see a dry toothbrush and a mouth with chocolate around the edges.*"

Concrete reporting and follow-through supports the developing brain's readiness to distinguish wish and reality, without the child picking up the message "I am bad," and without feeling labeled as a "liar."

*Follow through so that the task gets done and this brand of storytelling doesn't become reinforced.

Follow-through: *"Let's go brush teeth now."*

Follow-through with extra support if the task, at that moment, is hard: *"We will have your story when your teeth are clean"* (this is a reminder of good things to come) or, *"Teddy doesn't know how to brush teeth, should we bring him along so you can show him how?"* (this brings companionship and pride in knowing how).

When There Is No Evidence

When there is **no evidence** to report or the who-did-what is unclear, report whatever piece you know to be true and the consequence of that truth: *"We had enough cookies for everyone, but now some are missing. That is a sad thing. Now we can't have cookies together,"* or, *"Someone forgot our rule about saving cookies for lunchtime. We can't bake cookies when it's too hard for everyone to remember our rule."*

With K+

By around age six, children are getting pretty good at distinguishing truth from imagination. Lying can become more complex in the older child, and while we can continue to report the wish, report the evidence, and follow through, we also have the benefit of added tools. With older children:

- We can also create an opportunity for the child to turn the lie around. One way to do this is to give the child a second chance without harsh judgment. For instance, begin a new sentence that the child can then complete with the truth: *"What I meant to say was…"*

- It is very important for adults to create logical consequences related to lying. Focus on the transgression that the lie was meant to cover up. For example, if the family rule is homework is done before TV and the child tells you he's done when in fact he isn't, then the logical consequence is that he has lost the TV privilege for at least one day.

Because many of us live in families with more than one child, it can feel unfair to a sibling not to have TV because of the actions of another. If the TV is in a general living area, this is an opportunity to acknowledge that, "As a family, we work together so everyone learns the important things."

- We can also discuss the concept of lying in a general way. This is more successful if you use examples that have nothing to do with your child's specific behavior. For example, if a character in a story lies, open it up for discussion (discussion, not lecture): *"Was she telling the truth? Why do you think she lied? What do you think will happen because of the lie?"* etc.

- Finally, if we really want our kids to value honesty, the best thing we can do is model honesty. As your child's understanding of the world becomes more complex, the act of modeling becomes even more important.

The Bigger, Better, Best Lie

In their social interactions, young children will often misrepresent reality. *(My playset is as big as a mountain!)* When you overhear these tall tales, most often the best thing to do is to let it go. This is also true, though harder to do, when the lie sounds less like an active imagination and more like bragging. *(My playset is bigger than yours.)*

While another preschooler may not challenge these statements, he may begin one of his own and you may find yourself refereeing a "no, mine's bigger!" contest. These status arguments are often defused by acknowledging that it is OK for each to like one's own best. On the other hand, kindergarten-plus children will often force peers to examine their statements of bigger, better, best. It would not be beyond another school-age child to actually measure it!

The reason why it is often best to let these tall tales go in the moment is that, especially for more sensitive children, the harm caused by embarrassment in front of a peer would outweigh the benefit, in that moment, of teaching about lying. Later—in private—to instill the difference between wish and reality you can say: *"I heard you talk about playsets. Do you wish we had a bigger playset?"* You can also support the child's understanding by choosing a bedtime story that night about the consequences of lying.

For children who are beginning to understand the disparity of economics, this is an opportunity to have a heart-to-heart conversation about how families make choices about the size of playsets. Do not, however, frame this discussion as "our family doesn't have the money for..." Not only can it place undue importance on money, young children can and do worry about such things! The news and stories from school that you may not know about can create fearfulness and added anxiety about whether there is enough money for the basic needs, not just bigger playsets.

WHEN IS LYING A CONCERN?

When a child—despite being old enough, mature enough, and having received effective and kind modeling and teaching—persists in lying, very often the lying is a sign of distress in the child's life, whether from anxiety or social pressures. If you are worried, consider the following questions:

- Does the child have the developmental maturity to understand the concept of honesty and to be fully conscious of lying? (Usually by age seven.)

- Does the child, in general, show impulse control similar to that of his or her peer group?

- Has honesty been modeled for the child and reinforced as a value?

- Has the child been unable to consistently benefit from lying?

- Is the child's lying serious, persistent, or interfering with the quality of the child's relationships (with you and/or others)?

An answer of NO to one or more of the above questions can point to where work may need to begin or where parental expectations may need adjusting. An answer of YES to all of the above suggests that the child's lying often indicates a need for professional intervention. Pediatricians, school counselors, and child psychologists will be able to help you determine the best course of action to support your child.

Children cannot fully realize the value of being honest and trustworthy, since these are abstract concepts that are defined by behavior over multiple life domains. By addressing lying as it occurs in preschool years, parents are demonstrating the need for children to adhere to family values. Continuing follow-through during the elementary school years reinforces positive life values.

THE PLAYGROUP
IS HARD WORK

Watching children in playgroup settings will give parents information about the skills they need to be able to participate fully in such interactions. The following are some brief descriptions of patterns adults may observe and some suggestions for corresponding supports that parents and group leaders can offer.

WANDERING	STRATEGY
This child walks around but does not stop to observe the play of others. He may drift from object to object or from play area to play area without engaging either with objects or with others.	Shadow in the role of playmate. Invite interest in objects first. Talk about them, ask the child what she notices about the object. As interest or engagement increases, add discussion about what others are doing.

ALOOFNESS	STRATEGY
It may look as though the child avoids others or is unwilling to make social contact.	Draw the child into cooperative play through simple non-competitive games that allow each child to participate, or provide large building materials and invite the child to join in the process.

ANXIOUSNESS	STRATEGY
Anxiety can be expressed through clinging, rigid body tone, repeated need for reassurance, or resistance to being left for even brief periods of time.	Build trust by giving the children and adults in the space names. Supply a verbal narrative of positive intent when peers approach. "Sam wants to see how the truck dumps." Nurture playfulness in your interactions with the child and nearby peers. Narrow the child's focus by engaging with materials or a small group of peers.

DABBLING	STRATEGY
Toddlers are natural dabblers, but as children move toward age three their attention spans are expected to increase so that they engage for longer periods of time. Rather than spending a few moments to touch or taste as a toddler might do, a child will spend time to manipulate an object or use it as an expression of imaginative play.	This strategy parallels that of the child who wanders. Move with the child. As they begin to dabble, share your attention through discussion—and when possible—join in the play with the objects to expand the amount of time the child will focus.

BEING IGNORED	STRATEGY
This may happen to a child who plays well on her own but seems to have no idea how to get involved with peers, or whose bids for entry into a group are ignored.	The social context may require adult coaching for both the ignored child and for the peers. Highly engaged children may miss a peer's request to join in. If this happens only rarely, then it is not a cause for concern. Simply encourage the child to try again or to find alternate peers or a different activity. (See Social-Emotional, page 40.) If, however, the child is consistently ignored, group leaders can support activities in which the child is given a group leadership opportunity.

REJECTION	STRATEGY
Peers will sometimes reject children with lower language skills or fewer positive social skills.	If rejection is based on behavior that makes other children feel unsafe, then a trusted adult must remain present during interaction with peers to guide and direct play. (See Playmates: From Shadowing to Coaching, page 46.) As trust is re-established and safety more assured, adults can begin to supervise from a little more distance. For other children, directly teach basic social skills through role playing, puppets or stories. Whenever possible, create the opportunity for social practice through one-on-one play.

PART III: PARENT & PERSON

THE ADVISORS: WHEN OTHER ADULTS ARE WELL-INTENTIONED

Other adults are directly engaged in our efforts to raise our children. It may be an unsolicited comment from a bystander, an invited discussion with a teacher, or advice from grandparents...whatever the context may be, being a parent means that you are likely to encounter the challenges of collaboration. At the core, our comfort with collaboration will be impacted by our answers to these questions:

Do I trust the other adult's positive intent? Any perceived threat to our young is likely to trigger a highly emotional response on our part. When other adults use words or tones that are sharp to our ears, we may be unable to hear their input in any kind of constructive way. Remember, if you cannot trust the other person's positive intent, you will not be able to engage that adult as part of the "village" that helps you raise your child.

Do I trust the other adult's skill? Historically, early childhood education and childcare providers have not been required to have the kind of training that would support skill development. Although this is changing, there may be settings in which child guidance skills may be called into question. For instance, church volunteers are expected to have loving intent, but may not be trained to manage groups of young children. Others, like librarians and pediatric office staff, may have great professional skill, yet still be surprised by the various behaviors of children.

> No one is expected to love and know your child as you do. However, there are cues in tone and words that will convey how your child is perceived. Negative perceptions will carry over beyond a single event.

How does the other adult see my child? When a child is having difficulty in a social setting that you are not a part of, such as preschool, it is important to listen closely to how the adult describes your child.

Do I need more information? Trust your gut as well as your intellect. For highly impulsive or intensely active children, it may be easy to believe they are the cause of social problems with both peers and adults. Before accepting this frame of reference, do a gut check. Examine the environment and pay attention to your reflections on the earlier questions in this section. It may be that the skill level of the adult or the environment are incongruent with your child's needs at the moment. It may be that the information you need is a professional developmental evaluation, or it may be that the child and adult temperaments are mismatched.

Do we share values and goals for the child? A teacher who sees the need for focused attention on letter sounds may not be the easiest collaborator for a parent whose goal is to increase a child's confidence in social interactions with peers. Closer to home, it may be that Mom and Dad are establishing rules and expectations different from those of the grandparents. Frank discussions about goals for children will help keep collaborating adults on the same page and help minimize misunderstandings.

FAMILY ADVISORS

Family is both a great gift and a great challenge. When working with grandparents, consider that just as we teach our children that they have choices in how to behave, we do too. Family traditions can extend to communication styles. Two examples of different common—but less productive—behavior patterns within the family are:

React rather than respond

When we're surprised by another's comment or behavior we can easily react rather than respond. Screaming at another adult may convey the general message that you don't like that person or what he or she did, but for children, overhearing this can create a climate of fear and does nothing to teach them more sophisticated social skills than they have already.

Say nothing and seethe

Although this may avoid immediate conflict, it will do nothing to support change. It is, however, appropriate to delay speaking to the other adult when you are angry or when it may cause the child to experience emotional distress to see two adults in conflict with one another.

With awareness of your own patterns and those of your family, you can develop an approach that works best for all involved. Here are some practical strategies and also some things to keep in mind that may help:

Plan ahead, together

To circumvent some of the less productive family patterns, co-parents can **plan as a team** before issues arise. Although we are often too hurried to have quiet discussions about our goals as parents and co-leaders in our family, it can be helpful to create non-confrontational discussion time with one another. Here are a couple of introductory discussion starters:

"You know your mom takes me by surprise when she gives the kids soda rather than milk or water. How would you like me to respond to her?"

"Our little ones are so active that I worry about the holidays with your folks. I'd like to buffer the pressure on your folks, the kids, and you and me. Got some ideas of ways we can make this work easier?"

Raising young children is often the first time a daughter will have to challenge her father's humor, or that an adult son will have to challenge his mother's approach to parenting. This sometimes difficult—but important—act can be a developmental milestone for both the individual and the family.

Remember that every couple has a cross-cultural experience of life. The norms of the family in which we grew up may be similar, but they are never the same as our partner's. We need shared values on which to build our families. This does not mean that there will be congruent expressions of those values. The better we understand the patterns of our partner's family, the better able we are to manage the stress of sharing the parenting roles and responsibilities.

Having developed a congruent picture of the family you want to create, when clarifying expectations involving an "in-law," it's recommended that the directly related adult speak to the "offending party" to help them understand the pattern expected. The son talks to his mother and father, not the daughter-in-law. The sister is the one to talk to her sibling, not the brother-in-law.

Speak to the child, not the adult

When children are old enough to know about family rules (usually around age three and above), it can be useful to direct the conversation to the child. Here are examples (and I'm sure you can envision the context).

"It looks as though Grandma doesn't know about the way we do it in our family. What does the clock tell us about bedtime at this house?"

"You know what? We forgot to tell Grandma about how we do desserts. Do you want to tell Grandma what our family rule is about how many desserts we have after supper?"

Pay attention to your inner story

At about age nine we begin to build the stories of our lives. Sometimes we are conscious of those stories, as in, "I'm good at math. I can learn about ratios and not worry." Or, "I know I'm doing a good job at work. I deserve to be in line for promotion." But more often than not we are building our life stories line-by-line with little thought to the big picture we're creating for our families and ourselves.

For example, that "happily ever after" story we had at the beginning of our relationship takes a hit when we press play on a negative storyline with phrases like "he always…" and "she never…" *Always* and *never* may be true for eye color, but few other human traits and behaviors are so permanent. Being aware of the emotions generated by our inner story allows us to consider when we need to ask more clearly for what we need, when we need to name feelings without accusation, or to listen to our bodies for cues to other needs.

Understand that we don't always think like grown-ups when we live our lives and tell our stories

We may have heard of the inner child, but we rarely stop to think about whether we are looking at our relationship and life story through a child's eye. Children are egocentric (*It's all about me!*) and engage in magical thinking (*Some people have magic powers to make things good or bad*). Checking in with ourselves to determine if we're too tired, hungry, or lonely—with the intent of taking care of ourselves—is an adult perspective. But being irritated and thinking, *If he loved me, he would know what I need,* or, *Can't she see I'm tired? I worked all week!* is actually a bit of leftover fairytale thinking in which The Magician is supposed to know how everyone thinks and feels and can provide everything needed to make it better.

Resist the "tyranny of the urgent"

Unfortunately, when you're a parent, an employee, or when you need a safe toy-free path through the living room, everything that needs you and needs taking care of is important. Because of this, we need to stay connected to what is deeply important. As we struggle with the importance of all the demands of life *and* the importance of individual care and time for our adult relationships, often it is the latter that gets lost. Sometimes we prioritize children's needs over other members of the family, rationalizing that an adult can wait. It is true; we do learn to wait our turn as we grow up. The risk, however, is that if the demand to wait is too often or too long, we can come to a point of deep disappointment, or even to a place in which we are too emotionally tired to care. Or equally sad, we come to a point of resenting those we love for having received so much while we were waiting so patiently for our turn.

Commiseration is not always support, and support is not always commiseration

Finally, our stories can be shaped by our friends and families. We benefit from the loyalty and love of others who know us. However, we need those important others to be friends of our primary relationship, too. It may help to remember that the others in our life will at times have their own child-view eyes, and perhaps want to take sides or add negative themes to our story.

There is no perfect formula for every issue that can arise in the effort to collaborate with other adults. Collaboration can challenge us and lead us out of our comfort zone, reminding us that children are not the only members of the family learning and growing. Challenging though it may be, the important lesson for children is not that adults are perfect, but that they will make the effort to follow the same "rules" we are teaching them. This may translate into taking better physical care of oneself, into taking moments for rest and relaxation, or into asking for professional help when collaboration seems out of reach.

PARENTS AND PARTNERS

Perhaps one of the hardest things for parents to work through is the balance of time children need, the time for tasks of running a household, and the need to still have time to be together. One way in which to consider the task of co-parenting is to note the patterns that are evolving or have evolved in the relationship since children entered the picture.

Couple-parenting dynamics often fall into three dominant patterns: traditional, egalitarian, and flexible.

Traditional

Although often, but not always, gender-based, family tasks are divided into those performed by the *out-of-the-home breadwinner* and the *home-front manager*. These designations are correlated to who makes decisions where. The home-front manager makes decisions about the home and the tasks within the home, while the out-of-the-home breadwinner makes decisions about the car, yard maintenance, and perhaps purchases not directly related to household needs. Cultural phrases that indicate a home-front manager "doesn't work" because they spend more time on the less visible home-front tasks and childcare create a context in which one partner's contribution to the family may be perceived as less valuable. Children of both genders who internalize this notion may face challenges in understanding and valuing themselves and their contributions as adults. Many modern couples carry an expectation of dual careers so that out-of-the-home breadwinner is a title that applies to both. If both partners don't also share or negotiate the role of home-front manager, one partner will be overburdened by double duties.

Egalitarian

Both members of the couple fulfill both traditional roles, evenly dividing the duties of out-of-the-home breadwinner and home-front manager. All decisions are shared. To many people this seems an ideal way in which to honor the value and contributions of each caring adult. Before children, this may indeed have been a highly satisfying model for a couple. However, when children are part of the family, the sheer number and pace of decisions involved in caring for children and running a household can create a climate of cognitive and emotional overwhelm.

Flexible

Childcare and management decisions are areas defined by the event. In this model, the adult who is present at the time makes decisions and reports to the other simply to share information rather than to seek approval or confirmation of the decisions and outcomes of the event. The success of this model depends on a well-developed set of common values, a great deal of trust in the partner, as well as confidence in the other's skill in dealing with all areas of heart and home.

If we think of the family as a team, each of these general patterns can be adapted by playing to each other's strengths. So that in a traditional model, the partner who is most often filling the breadwinner role may actually be best at getting a child to settle for sleep, so will take on that duty although it is "traditionally" a home-front manager responsibility. Or a usually egalitarian or flexible team may create a smoother evening flow if one partner focuses on childcare to free the other for cooking.

Whatever the model, adults are called to consider the ways in which they may be verbally or non-verbally undermining the other parent. Although it does not immediately sound negative, phrases like, "*Dad babysits on Tuesday nights*" place him in a role of temporary help rather than acknowledging his full responsibility as a co-parent.

Even when there is a rhythm to childcare and household tasks that seems to be working for the family, adults can feel as though something is missing. Often this is related either to limited self-care, limited couple-care, or both. It can be a creative challenge to figure out self-care when faced with the needs of vulnerable children. However, the basics of care hold true for adults as well as children: good nutrition, appropriate activity/exercise, rest and relaxation. Using these three categories as a basis, here are some suggestions.

NUTRITION

Whether we use the old food group model or the newer My Plate recommendations from the U.S. Department of Agriculture (www.choosemyplate.gov), most adults have figured out what they *should* eat. One quick self-check about our eating is to ask ourselves whether we would offer our children this food and, if so, how much? It can be amazing how much more aware we are of the decisions we make to care for children than those we make to care for ourselves. If your *child within* is hungry, consider eating at least as well as you feed your children.

ACTIVITY AND EXERCISE

In the same manner, children are almost always active throughout their day. A toddler may find it difficult to sit still long enough to eat! As toddlers grow into preschoolers they may be able to sit longer, but still find ways to enjoy play that engages the whole body.

Although many parents are active just trying to keep up with children and chores, this level of activity may not bring refreshment or raise spirits in the same way the endorphins of a good run can. Maintaining a fitness regimen may be particularly difficult in inclement weather or when children are sick. To creatively manage these challenges may mean that parents have dance parties with their children or join games of tag, so that rather than watching children play, adults are actively playing with them. More than an investment in physical health, this is an investment in healthy attachment. Shared activity can also set a tone of joyfulness in the family.

REST AND RELAXATION

Because children's sleep may be irregular, rest and relaxation may seem like a mirage in a desert of nights of broken sleep. Unfortunately, for many adults this is compounded by the desire to "treat themselves" to other activities after the children are asleep, whether it be mundane chores, media indulgence or creative endeavors. An occasional late night will not cost significant physical or emotional well-being, but a regular pattern of short sleep is likely to result in physical and emotional distress—shorter temper, lower tolerance for frustration and illness—none of which contributes to being a good parent or life-companion. Again, when an adult uses a self-check of, "Would I encourage this choice for my children?" it may bring clarity to the need to prioritize sleep and relaxation.

RELATIONSHIP CARE

Couple-care cannot be left out of the discussion of good self-care. Judith Wallerstein, author of *The Good Marriage*, has said that the adult primary relationship is a living member of the family and *needs and deserves care every day*. Although a weekly night out is a great opportunity for couples to relax and enjoy each other, fifteen minutes a day of checking in with one another is the minimum daily requirement for maintaining basic couple well-being. If during this fifteen minutes there is a back rub or foot massage, so much the better for maintaining nurturing touch during this highly demanding stage of family development.

SEXUALITY

Ready or not, children may surprise parents by exploration of their bodies, questions about babies, or giggling about body functions and noises. For worried parents, it may be helpful to understand that conversations about human sexuality begin simply. Over several years, additional conversations will provide more information and the context for making values-based decisions. The following will offer a brief overview of the nature of family conversation about human sexuality, and then return to a focus on preschool children.

We begin first by giving children the names of all their body parts. Envision a child singing the simple body naming song "Head, Shoulders, Knees and Toes." It is light and fun, but it skips over even the most nonthreatening names of torso, chest and navel. Perhaps they were omitted because they are hard to rhyme. But, when thinking about cultural patterns it is interesting to note that body parts from neck to hips are much more likely to be given no names or called cutesy names than are other body features like ears, elbows, ankles and toes.

In parallel with learning the words for their bodies are the social skills that help children accept, express, and implement basic rules of interaction with others. Learning about boundaries, where my body ends and yours begins, and the right of the other to be heard and honored during social interactions become the other basics that underlie mature expressions of sexuality.

After the initial vocabulary of human bodies is in place, early elementary children will have matured to a rigid sense of what is right and what is wrong in relationship to their bodies based on the answers Mom, Dad, and teacher have given about acceptable behavior.

In middle elementary the ability to "think about my thinking" (meta-cognition) develops, and along with it the ability to understand that context has a part in decision-making. Meta-cognition includes the ability to understand that feelings provide information about one's self in relationship to others. During this stage of development there will be both peer support and pressure for values-based (moral) decision-making across broad areas of the child's life like academic success, dress, and participation in extracurricular activities. Practice in these less emotionally charged arenas lay a framework for later decisions about expressing personal sexuality.

Broadly, for children of all ages to develop healthy attitudes and behaviors toward human sexuality, we need to encourage children and ourselves to:

- Tell the truth

- Know the facts

- Do no harm to yourself or others

- Consider the feelings of others

- Consider your own feelings

When living with preschool children it may help to remember there's so much for preschoolers to learn! The basics of sexuality are just one more part of life for them. Their normal curiosity and lack of social inhibition can create some really awkward moments for the adults in their lives. It may reassure parents to have some sense of what to expect.

Do expect:

- Curiosity about differences between male and female bodies

- Questions about where babies come from, especially if the family is expecting a new sibling or age-mates are having new siblings

- Interest in Mom's breasts, especially if she is nursing a younger sibling

- Interest in pregnant women and new babies

- Holding genitals if bored or under stress

- Touching genitals either for comfort or for sensation

- Giggles and jokes about bathroom functions

- Participation in "show me" or "doctor" play

- Fascination with baby diaper changes, or bathroom activities of others

- Interest in seeing Mom or Dad undress

Talking birds and bees is different than discussing sexuality with children. Plants, birds, and bees really are different from people in how they make more plants, birds, and bees. It is fun for children to know that most plants create seeds, that birds lay a limited number of eggs, and that bees have a queen that lays many, many eggs. It is important that they know that women and girls have ova and men and boys have sperm. It is simply more information about how the world works.

Explanations need to be kept simple and clear. Asking a child what they think can also help a parent to know where to begin. A question like, "How do mommas get babies?" can turn into a discussion that begins with a question of your own. "What do you think?" You may be surprised to hear that they think mommas get babies from a store (after all, from their experience, stores are where you get everything else, and they do see many babies in shopping carts). An explanation can be honest without being complicated. "Babies start to grow when sperm from a daddy meets an ovum from a momma. They grow in a special part of a mom's body called a uterus. When babies are big enough to know how to breathe they come out through a place on a mom's body called a vagina."

Having said all that, will the child really understand all it means? Not likely, but what you have conveyed is basic/accurate information, openness to their questions, and an attitude that sexuality is another part of who we are as people. They may let the topic rest for a while or they may continue to ask for the same explanation. There are age-appropriate books available to help satisfy curiosity about parts of the body we cannot see.

Children caught playing "show me" or "doctor" provide parents and caregivers with what educators call a "teachable moment"—awkward, but valuable. This kind of play indicates interest, a time to teach respect of every person's body privacy (boundaries), and an opportunity to answer questions. When interrupting sex play, it is important to avoid responding with harsh tones, blaming, or other reactions that create fear. Masturbating is another opportunity to help children learn that it is a behavior done in the privacy of their room.

If a parent feels that any behavior is excessive, it may indicate a time to look for underlying reasons.

PROTECTING YOUR CHILD

One of the most difficult topics for a parent to consider is the risk of child abuse or molestation. News reports of child abductions and flagrant abuses of power in schools or churches can make parents question their ability to keep children safe in even the most child-centered environment. This may be especially true for parents who themselves were abused and/or molested as children.

Admonitions such as "Don't talk to strangers" do not help children understand how to seek help if they become separated from their parents—because if everyone is a stranger, who can they ask for help? Nor does this blanket rule offer children any tools for dealing with situations that feel uncomfortable to them. But parents actually have several paths of instruction to protect their children—without stoking fears.

Teach what to do if they need help

Although parents do their best to train children to stay with them when they shop or go to large events, still there are times when children may inadvertently become separated from family members. In such cases, it is important that children know how to seek help. Research tells us that young children cannot easily distinguish the various forms of uniforms. This presents a problem if our instructions to them are "find a police man or woman" (even if one were in sight, they may not recognize the police uniform as different than the uniform of the janitorial service).

Today, parents are recommended to tell their young child to "find another mommy." If they are lost, they should look for a woman with young children. The parent should contact store staff immediately to signal a Code Adam. This will limit the possibility of the child leaving or being taken out of the building.

Children need to know their full name, and their parents' names (beyond Momma and Daddy). A simple song or marching rhythm can help preschoolers learn to recite their full name and address. Some even memorize phone numbers.

Teach about strangers

A cute smile invites many a stranger to speak to a child in the seat of a shopping cart. What's a parent to do when you recognize that the senior citizen waiting next in line is no threat, yet you want to ensure a model of safety? One strategy is to teach the child instructions for when it *is OK* to talk to a stranger. This means being clear that the child has permission to talk to another adult when Momma or Daddy is with them.

Then comes the hard part. Teach resistance to the common strategies abductors use to lure children.

- Teach children to avoid *strangers who approach them for help* to find lost puppies, figure out directions, or any other request for help. *Remind children that strangers should be asking another adult!*

- Teach them to ask you first before accepting anything from someone who offers candy or treats.

- Teach them a secret family code word and that anyone who tells them, "Your mommy or daddy sent me to pick you up from school," will also be able to say this code word. This code word should be something your child finds fun and easy to remember. You and your children can think together and choose something you know is a special thing to think about, like sticky waffles or long-necked giraffes and purple dinosaurs.

Teach children about personal boundaries

Unfortunately, most people who abuse children are known to the child and the family. They may be family members, friends of the family, or have roles that give them special access to children.

Many of us can remember from our childhood being encouraged to "give a hug or kiss" to a relative or family friend. When children are hesitant to approach or to offer these kinds of signs of affection, reassure them that it is OK to decide if and when it's time to hug or kiss someone. You may have to be your child's advocate with an offended relative. As an alternative to more intimate contact, you might teach them lighter ways to signal affection and honor boundaries—like high fives or fist bumps.

Teach children they can trust their internal knowing

One very thoughtful parent described talking with children about that "feeling they get in their stomach." This is particularly meaningful as a teaching experience in discussion about the way our stomachs feel when we're with friends, when we meet someone new, when we like our teacher, or when we're worried about something.

As children become older they will better understand the sense of "intuition" that is often the best cue we receive that it's wise to stop and pay attention. Having said this, every parent knows their child best, and this intuitive warning system may work better in some children than others.

Teach about sex

Different families will have different practices about naming body parts. One approach that is easy for a very young child to understand is to use terms like "swimsuit area" as a way to define private areas of the body. Teach them that they have the right to say NO to anyone who wants to touch or play "secret" games with their bodies. "Tell us if something happens" is important for you to say to your child, but remember that if he or she has been intimidated or threatened, it may be difficult to speak up. This is why it is often more empowering to teach them that inappropriate touching and secret body games are "*against the law!*" Children are very literal thinkers and need to have a clear understanding that there are rules that say that "big people" are not allowed to "play" in this way with children. This will help them to feel more confident that reporting an interaction is the right thing to do.

Give children accurate names for all their body parts. It is amazing that we never hesitate to name body parts like head, shoulders, knees and toes, and yet we give "cutesy" names or no names at all for whole sections of our bodies. The risk of this kind of cultural pattern is that it signals that some parts of the body are less OK than others, and it leaves children and adults with no vocabulary to discuss body safety.

Remain vigilant

Although there is much we can do to teach children about personal safety, it is still important to remain vigilant of others in our children's lives.

- Note the physical environment so that children are easily observed when working one-on-one with another adult. For example, for older children, some music practice rooms have solid doors, are soundproofed, and placed at the rear of a store. Recognizing this environment as a potential high-risk setting allows the parent to make a choice of safety over convenience.

- Note if your child's playmate has older siblings or other family guests who are left unsupervised with the younger children as they play. You will need to know and trust these others as much as you do the original hosts.

- Note any adults who seem to pay special attention to a particular child to the exclusion of others in the family.

- Note any adults who consistently are especially interested in joining the children when at multi-age social events, rather than interacting with the adults.

- Be aware that most abuse is perpetrated by someone the victim knows or is related to.

- Counter mythologies with evidence-based knowledge:

  ○ Sex offender registries cover a broad array of crimes. For example, there is no distinction between a pedophile and someone who once sent a "sext" as a nineteen-year-old. People can be on these lists for a lifetime. For these reasons, the list on its own, without context, does not automatically indicate a danger and may distract from real dangers in children's lives (see above).

  ○ Sex offender registries list those who have been caught, but do nothing to identify others.

  ○ According to the Bureau of Justice Statistics, sex offenders are one of the least likely groups to be rearrested for the same offense. *

  ○ *Reported* sexual and physical abuse of children has declined 62% and 56% respectively between 1992 and 2010. Though the majority of sex offenses still go unreported, findings from the National Child Abuse and Neglect Data System (NCANDS) support that the reported statistics reflect a true decline in prevalence. **

Err on the side of safety

Children only have one childhood in which to feel safe and secure.

While it's important to have the most accurate information, we understand that statistics are only so helpful when it comes to the safety and well-being of children. One additional risk to the overall health of families and communities is that in the face of our vigilance, men have reported that they will not touch or engage with children and that they feel vulnerable if they happen to be alone with other people's children because they are afraid of being wrongly accused. It is one thing to create policies that buffer risks, like background checks for church volunteers, and quite another to create a context that deprives children of positive adult engagement.

---

* Bureau of Justice Statistics Special Report NCJ 193427 https://www.bjs.gov/content/pub/pdf/rpr94.pdf.

** https://www.nsopw.gov/en-US/Education/FactsStatistics.

PEERS AND PEER PRESSURE— THEIRS AND OURS

A big part of the playgroup and school experience is learning about and with peers. It is often through peer relationships that children learn more about the world. Sometimes they learn through the joy of friendships, other times through pressure they might not otherwise experience. Few people are cued to consider peer pressure as relevant for families of young children, instead focusing more on the power of peer pressure for older children and teens. While concern about peer pressure for older children is understandable, it is helpful to remain mindful of the peer pressure we experience ourselves. It is also helpful to be aware of how some forms of peer pressure can be positive in the lives of individuals, families, and communities.

PEER PRESSURE

Do you notice peer pressure in your own experiences? As a parent, have you ever bought something for your child because another playmate has one and you feel "pressure" to get your child one too? Do you feel some pressure to keep your yard up to the standard set by others? Do you feel disappointment in a neighbor who does not? The phrase "keeping up with the Joneses" is an acknowledgment that adults also face peer pressure. Some of the "keeping up" reflects positive peer pressure, some clearly less so.

Peer pressure is positive when it is supportive of (or congruent with) a value base that benefits the individual as well as the community. For example, positive peer pressure can be seen in playgroups in which the adult members actively support one another in maintaining verbally and physically non-violent interactions with young children.

There is, of course, always the potential for "keeping down with the Joneses"—say, for example, that a certain group accepts the idea that children be parented at the top of adult voices or left for long periods without adult supervision. Whether the group accepts this as a result of negative peer pressure or simply a lack of positive peer pressure is open for discussion. Both examples are offered simply to acknowledge that there is a **power** within individuals and within communities to create a context for the lives of others. **Becoming aware of peer pressure and naming it returns the power to you.**

PRESCHOOLERS

At this age, a child's perception of peers or friends can often be defined as someone who is available to play or someone who has something they want to play with. This is age-appropriate ego-centric behavior and friendship understanding.

- **Interests and friendships are still developing.** Playing in a variety of spaces outside the home with different kinds of resources allows the child to explore without placing a burden on the household to have everything that might be of interest.

- **Remember that support need not be expensive.** If your child really likes the play kitchen at a friend's home, it does not mean that you must have one too. If your play-space or budget simply cannot manage a large piece of equipment, do not feel as though you are failing your little one! Enjoying the play at the friend's house can often be enough. And if the interest remains strong, you can adapt a drawer or shelf in your kitchen to hold smaller child-size tools and engage your child in safe family food preparation.

- **Focus on your family and individual strengths.** If your home has great outside space and limited inside space, then focus on using the outside space to your child's advantage. A corner of the yard for mud pie/sandbox cooking can be satisfying. Sidewalk chalk for roads or pictures can support the active imagination of a child who may be limited to deck play. If you are great at exploring art or craft options with young children, then claim that strength and support their gross motor skills in other ways like trips to the local park. Parents do not need to compare their resources to others. When they tailor what they have to the developmental needs of children—large and small muscle activity, consistent love and care—they can be satisfied their children can and will do well.

KINDERGARTEN+

This is an age of shared work. Children are beginning to differentiate friends by shared interests. They can and do compare themselves with others and judge when someone is "better than me at ___."

- **Part of their developmental work is to notice, compare, categorize and choose.** Children will begin to cluster in friendship groups that reflect their budding skills at sports, music, games, or that develop out of mutual friends. Some of their interests and skills will likely need to be supported by investing in "stuff"—a baseball bat, drumsticks, shin guards, or game-playing cards, for example. One value-based process that may place you as a parent in high contrast to other parents is to model for your children that their "needs" will be met, but that new is not necessary. Some creative parents, when faced with adult peer pressure to buy new things, have created unique alternatives such as equipment exchange fairs that allow everyone to benefit.

- **Classroom reading and service projects give context for economic decisions.** Participation in school and community projects will often begin to provide opportunities for children to better understand and become increasingly aware of the differences in economic well-being, and the great variety in people's living circumstances.

- **Children need you to do direct teaching of your family values as well as the "whys" underlying your choices.** Helping children begin to understand the "rules your family uses" for what to buy and when to buy it is challenging. Money is an abstract concept. For children under eight, their early understanding of numbers and dollar values will complicate even simple purchases made with gift money. It can be a worthwhile but very difficult lesson to help them face the disappointment that their limited funds will not buy their newest desire. It helps at times to provide three options for a child to choose from rather than have them experience the aisles of a store and sort from so large a set of options. One note of caution: while telling a child, "we don't have enough money for…" may technically be true, using this language when teaching can potentially create fear about having enough for basic needs vs. wants. Simply accepting your role as family leader with language like "the momma and daddy in this family aren't ready to buy…" or changing it to something like "our family spends money differently than other families" supports an understanding of family boundaries as well as family values.

- **Children need you to support them as they face peer pressure in friendships.** A child who always defers to a friend's choice of what to play may need help to know how to state his preferences to someone other than immediate family. Pointing out a process as simple as turn taking may open the door. For example, saying to your child's friend, "Last time you came to visit you picked playing dolls; this time it's Sally's turn to choose what to play first." This kind of simple guideline can help both children to understand that reciprocity is a part of friendship.

As children grow they are moving into a much stronger socio-centric understanding. Parents recognize this in phrases like, "But Mom, nobody wears ___!" Often socio-centric children won't know what they want until they have examined what others have or do. Parents can help by encouraging **gentle self-reflection** *on their choices of clothes, friends, etc.*

- **If a child is pressuring you for a purchase, she may be reflecting her sense that she needs a particular prop to feel even with a peer.** Gentle questions about where the child's desire for an expensive purchase comes from will help you understand whether or not this purchase is something you can support by helping to create an opportunity for her to earn it. Her uncertainty regarding group status may not immediately go away, but the process of earning something through individual effort supports the development of healthy self-esteem. It can also help some children to value and care for the objects they have earned.

- **Early adopters of trendy items can create social pressure on children and families.** One of the most recent examples of early adopter pressure can be seen in the number of children who have individual cell phones. Adult cell phone owners soon found the advantages of easy access to one another and presumed that this same benefit would serve them as parents with access to their children. No one foresaw this seemingly benign intent being exploited by things like sexting (sending explicit photos) or the impact of social bullying through technology. The difficult lesson here for all parents is that we cannot always predict how our children will use what we provide to them. Even usually trustworthy children will continue to need adult supervision and support to address peer suggestions and pressures.

- **Help children understand their choices.** When we create opportunities for children to become self-reflective, they are better able to withstand the negative pressure from peers and culture.

ADULTS

This is a time in which we are called to clarify and live by our values. Other adults, e.g., friends, grandparents, can bring a form of social pressure through their expectations as well as through their actions. Conversations with a co-parent or trusted friend may help to clarify when to speak or draw a boundary to address external social pressure.

- **Trust your gut!** If making a purchase or saying yes to an invitation makes you twinge, stop and think about why you might be considering it.

- **Practice saying calm, firm "NOs."** This is harder than one might think. Often women have been taught from childhood that saying no is impolite, or that it might hurt another's feelings. This kind of training can place women at physical and emotional risk. If you feel awkward saying "No," literally stand at a mirror and watch your face and body language. Imagine a setting in which you might feel pressure to say yes—for example, an invitation to a friend's sales party—and envision her subtle or not subtle pressure at your refusal. Continue to practice until your body language and voice are congruent with your intent to say "No."

- **Find others who reflect the values you hope to live.** Sometimes our families, immediate neighbors, and parents of our children's friends simply cannot be our best support. It takes effort to build a friendship network, but it is worth the effort. In addition to support for living our values, a positive friendship network can provide physical and emotional safety in times of individual or family crisis.

Each of us is faced with social pressure of some kind or another. This pressure is not always a negative. A preschool child reminded by a peer to take his thumb out of his mouth may be experiencing positive peer pressure that contributes to overall oral health. Thinking for ourselves within our social context and discovering comfort with our choices will lay the framework from which we can help our children with this major life assignment.

Remember that there is a **power** within individuals and within communities to create a context for the lives of others. **As we become aware of peer pressure—and name it—we are able to return the power to ourselves and our children.**

THE BUMPY DAY

We live in a hurried world. Sometimes we just want children to do what we say, when we say it. But if we raise children who are conditioned to having others think and decide for them, they will be less likely to be able to think and decide for themselves as teens or adults. Preschool children are just beginning to face the challenges of thinking and deciding for themselves (including accepting consequences). Understanding their concrete thinking, continuing development, and their beginning ability to problem solve can lessen the challenges of the day.

We parent with our whole bodies. This is important to remember when we find that words alone are not enough.

Day to day our parenting bodies:

Support attention. We often wrap our bodies around our children to support focus and settling. This is especially true when sharing favorite books at bedtime. It is not only our words that bring interest and engagement in the abstract world of children's books; our bodies have narrowed the world to a space of love and shared enjoyment. When we need to teach and guide, our touch can be equally effective to calm (assuming we remain calm) and settle an upset child.

Boundaries. Adult bodies help define boundaries of safe play and positive behavior. One firmly placed arm can act like a railroad barrier, preventing a "snatch-and-run" strategy for dealing with a sibling. Standing at the foot of a slide will keep children from running in the path of another landing child. Sometimes physical nearness itself is beneficial, as young children seem to borrow from the steady presence of an adult.

Meaning. Children read our bodies long before they can read a book! Body cues are often a child's most reliable source of information. Dad can tell his upset child that "everything is all right," but if Dad's body is rigid and agitated, the child gets the message: everything is *not* all right. Dad's agitation may be from being tired, but the child thinks that he too believes in the monster under the bed.

The abstract nature of some words is clarified through the calm, steady presence of our bodies. For example, yelling instructions from the other room, or giving instructions while you're distracted by other activity often leads to parental frustration and the classic phrase, "How many times do I have to tell you!" On the other hand, being close and making eye contact help confirm not only that you have the child's attention, but also that you intend that the instructions are to be attended to. They are not just more sounds in the background of a humming household.

For preschool children, there are times when meaning is reinforced by asking them to repeat the instruction. The question *"What did Mom tell you?"* requires multiple levels of thought to answer it—attention, memory, and picturing the in-structions. The answer may honestly be *"I don't know,"* because you didn't have the child's full attention at the time you said it, or the child may not remember or may not have pictured the meaning of the instruction. Your presence can support the child at any of these junctures, and if they don't remember what was said, it's time to repeat the instruction and try again.

We've been talking about your body parenting—your presence in the child's space. At times, your face may be more powerful than you know. For a child who appears overloaded (possibly, avoidant) of direct face-to-face leadership, your body can literally stand alongside him as you offer guidance. Placing your arm around a child's shoulders while you speak in lower tones to his ear may, for such children, be the best way to support attention during child guidance.

Active young children demand a lot of our parental time and energy. To also focus your attention on how you parent physically may feel like "one more thing" to add to your potential overload. But you may be surprised. When we know the value of bringing our bodies, not simply our words, to the tasks of child guidance, we can reduce the time and energy we spend correcting child behavior. Although communication is often first thought of as words, your body's presence may be a shortcut to improved communication.

It can be helpful to remember that small shifts make big differences. Your answers to the questions below may give you more power to manage the bumps during the day.

1. Do I have my child's attention before giving instructions?

2. Have I described the behavior the child needs to change? (A simple de-scription such as, "I see a boy jumping on the sofa," will help bring his

awareness to his behavior and could help him to self-guide before you guide the change.)

3. Have I used "when…then…" to describe the flow of activity? (Remember that "if you…" and "don'ts" can invite a power struggle.)

4. Have I created a mental picture of the positive behavior? (It is more helpful to tell a child, "Remember, you will hold Mom's hand in the parking lot when we get out of the car," than to tell her, "Don't run when we get out of the car.")

5. Have I planned our outings to fit my child's need for rest, food, and stimulation? (Missing sleep, late meals, and boredom are difficult for all ages.)

6. Have I looked at the outing through my child's eyes?

7. Have I cared for myself? (A rested and fed parent has more emotional and physical reserves to bring to the day.)

LABELS
IMPACT LIFE

As children begin to develop a sense of self we encounter the issue of labels and labeling. Often labels are communication shortcuts that are applied to young children early in our relationships with them. For example, "Drama Queen" may be short for a child who reacts with intensity to emotions. The term "Bully," applied to a preschool child, may be a reference to a highly active child who first uses body power rather than words in social problem-solving.

Often when we talk about using labels in families we focus on the harm done by labels that are obviously negative, such as: "Biter," "Whiner," or "Drama Queen." The first difficulty with a negative label is that using it as a "name" for the child implies that it is a trait rather than an indication of an area in which skills still need to be learned. A trait like left-handedness will not change. But with guidance and support, children will learn new skills for dealing with emotions and improving social interactions with others. So to "name" them a "Biter" early on implies that they will always be a "Biter," when in fact that's just not true. The additional difficulty with conversations that are focused on negative labels is that adults seem to ignore exploring the impact of labels that are not overtly negative. However, these labels may also have important consequences.

To explore the impact of a seemingly positive label, envision an encounter with a magic fairy who promised wonderful things if you would only put your child in a box. Would you put your child in a box?

Before you shout, "Of course not!" what if she told you, "It's a beautiful box and others will envy you and your child in that wonderful box"? Still hesitant? What if she told you that being in that box will be good for your child: This particular box has within it the promise that your child will have school success and, in the future, a great job. Living in the box promises a successful, fulfilling life!

It gets harder to say no in the face of all those promises, but if you have any experience with fairytales your gut is twinging.

In reality, you would be very wise to avoid this box. The fairy didn't mention that this box is the label "Smart" and that the promises are false. Think for a moment about children seen as "Underachievers." "These children are Smart!" teachers and parents exclaim. "Why aren't they living up to their potential?" If anything, these smart children now have another box with a different name, "Underachiever," and it isn't nearly as pretty or enviable as the first box.

You can see how the label "Smart" allows us to set up expectations and then offers us the opportunity to add another label when a child doesn't meet those expectations. Somehow the adults and children are caught in a sticky label trap. How did we ever get into this process in the first place?

Adults around a child use the word "smart" because we see the end product of the child's **time, attention, and practice.** Because the learning work of a toddler and preschooler is disguised as play, the time, attention, and practice may be harder for an adult to recognize. Further, because it is play, it is a joyful activity for the child. The added pleasure and attention from the parent or caregiver is a bonus to an already satisfying experience. As this pattern continues, children can internalize that "smart" means their experience of learning should be as easy as P.I.E.—Perfect, Instant, and Easy—or at least fun!

So, what makes a "Smart" child an "Underachiever"? Some presume that it may be an expression of anxiety. Why should a smart child be anxious about learning? Perhaps because for kindergarten+ children there is a newly developing inner voice that begins to ask, "Will the people who are important in my life be disappointed in me?" Or, equally powerful, this inner comparison may expand to setting what an adult might call an unrealistic expectation—Perfection.

For those who believe that smart people learn instantly, it may be an easy but erroneous logical next-step to accept that when answers don't come instantly, or at least as fast as their classroom neighbor, it's because "I'm just not smart enough." It's almost as though the learner has an image of her own "Smart" as an object that can be measured against the size of the task and seen as big enough to succeed or too little to bother. After all, in a recipe, if the cook only has half the flour needed for a cake, the best she can create is a half a cake. If a whole cake was the goal, it may not be worth the effort to begin.

Learning theorists suggest that **the amount and depth of learning is often the result of the amount of time focused on the content or skill.**

Shall we also mention that one understanding of procrastination—a behavioral pattern seen in some "Underachievers"—is an attempt by "discouraged perfectionists" to create a reason for why something is less than perfect? After all, they think, *If I had spent more time then it would have been better/perfect.*

Finally, from the inner experience of a learner, school assignments may not feel particularly easy or fun. For example, the added stress for children with limited handwriting skills that won't keep up with the story in their head makes a written assignment less joyful. It takes active support on the part of parents and teachers to help children faced with this kind of hurdle. Learning disabilities may be missed when labels get in the way of looking for other issues related to academic success.

People do, however, have unique aptitudes and interests. It is likely that basic aptitude and interest can make *the initial introduction to new content* rewarding to the learner. However, for anyone who has met an expert in any field, you quickly realize that the expert has spent a significant amount of time and attention engaging in the practices that make one an expert.

Lest we begin to think labels are only an issue for children at the point of developing a sense of self, consider the life impact that can result from childhood labels. Take for example adult learners who have been "Smart" enough to successfully manage their lives in so many other ways, who do not trust themselves to be smart enough to meet the goal of a new certification or degree. When faced with the perceived limitations of labels, movement away from artificial and somewhat obscure standards (for example, letter grades) toward a sense of individual mastery is often helpful. Children and adults can then focus their attention on the skills, time, and practice that the task requires, rather than holding themselves back by the focus on whether or not they are "Smart" enough.

BULLY   SPOILED   WHINER

DUMMY   LOUDMOUTH

WIMP

BRAT   DRAMA QUEEN

PART IV:
SO MUCH MORE

THE PRESCHOOL DECISION

To preschool, or not to preschool, that is the question. And if yes, then which one?

The decision of whether or not to send a child to preschool can be impacted by a variety of family circumstances as well as parental goals for young children. If the decision is *No* or *Not right now*, parents need to be aware that there are some social skills that require practice in small groups and access to children at or near the same age.

Preschools and other small group settings allow children to practice managing their bodies; begin to figure out the rules for collaborative interactions; practice listening and responding to leadership from other adults; and have the opportunity to expand their network of trusted adults and potential friends. *No* or *not right now* means that parents will need to consider how to provide these practice opportunities in other settings. (See *Social-Emotional* section, page 40.)

For those who have decided *Yes* to preschool, the next question is which one. This section shares information that can help you make that decision.

CHOOSING A PRESCHOOL

Check the school's licensing and credentials. There are requirements that licensed preschools must meet for health, safety, and teacher training.

Plan to visit more than one site. Take your child with you. You will gain much by seeing the materials available and watching the children and teachers together.

Pay attention to the following; any item can affect the quality of the experience you and your child will have:

- The teacher-child ratio (set by state standards)

- The temperaments and styles of the teachers

- The emotional and physical environment

- The philosophy of the preschool program

- The contract, including cost and expectations of parents (e.g., classroom volunteer time, or requests to provide snacks)

- The quality of the communication between you and the teacher(s) and director

One does not need to be a child development specialist to make positive judgments about learning environments and the potential "goodness-of-fit" for the child in your life. There is much that can be learned by taking time to observe a preschool in action.

Often observations begin with the "big picture" of the classroom in action. Take a few moments to focus on the various elements that provide the context for learning.

- Space for learning areas to balance active and quiet activities
- Safe, fun outdoor area
- Activities suitable for the age of the child
- Sufficient toys, books, and materials
- Clean, bright setting
- Children enjoying themselves
- Children and teachers working cooperatively in projects and in problem-solving
- The daily schedule
- The ways in which teachers work with children who do not want to participate

No observation would be complete without paying attention to the teacher(s) and the ways in which she or he embodies the role of classroom leader and child nurturer.

- Face (warm, loving) and voice (calm, soothing, cheerful, strong but caring)
- Gets down to children's level to talk or work with them
- Expresses enjoyment of children
- Evidence of good health practices, for example, hand washing
- Uses positive disciplinary methods (not harsh or frightening)
- Positive words and actions, not only when leading content, but in general interactions with children and co-leaders
- Gives children choices

- Encourages children to help themselves

After you've chosen:

- Communicate regularly with the teacher(s)
    - Determine the best method of communication (email, student notebooks, bulletin boards, notes in student bags)*
- Express any concerns early. Do not let them accumulate.
- Share information about your child.
- Be prompt for drop-off and pick-up times
- Stay involved

Just as early interactions with parents lay a foundation for attachment, we hope for every young child that their experience of preschool—teachers, peers, environment—lays a positive cognitive, emotional, and problem-solving foundation on which to build. From childhood story time to adult boardrooms, we encounter various forms of cognitively and physically challenging tasks that require collaborative groups. Often the social skills we use in these contexts began to develop in our early learning opportunities.

*Communication: Avoid classroom doorway conversations about concerns or particular behavior. These conversations distract the teacher from supporting all children entering or leaving the room. They distract the parent and child from any positive rituals of reattachment. And, further, young children are emotionally quick to expand your concern about a "bad" behavior to a sense of being a "bad" child.

GETTING READY TO READ

The elementary years are expected to be a time when children gain skill and competence in reading. However, the building blocks for reading are laid even earlier, primarily through conversation and shared reading experiences.

If parents spend too much of their parent-child time engaged with their electronic devices, they are depriving their children of a deep reservoir of words and discussions from which to build reading skills. Furthermore, a child's attachment is the primary building block for lifelong mental health. Healthy attachment requires we spend quality time as well as quantity time in interaction with those we love. Being with someone who is there but not "there" is a painful experience even for adults.

TALK TOGETHER

A child's speaking and listening skills develop in many fun ways. Even the least talkative parents sow the seeds for reading —from day one—by greeting babies with smiles and words. Playing with infants and toddlers, describing their world and naming the things they have in their hands, singing rhyming songs that help differentiate the meaning of similar-sounding words—all of these activities work to expand a child's ability to comprehend the stories that come later.

Reading preparation is based on knowing and understanding language. The biggest support for preparing children for reading is parent talk and parent-child conversations about... EVERYTHING.

READ TOGETHER

Although adults may see small people and their curious fingers and mouths as destructive to books, it's important to create an atmosphere of accessibility and fun around books. A sense of love and comfort is associated with reading when a child snuggles in Mom or Dad's lap to look at pictures and hear stories. A sense of excitement about books develops when those same people use different voices for characters and make the sounds of all the animals in the picture books. Through these interactions, children learn that books are part of play, and it won't be long before they join in the sounds and play of reading together.

Some of our highly active children will engage more fully if parents not only indicate different characters by changing their voices, but also use other verbal cues to contrast characters and events such as speeding up and slowing down, speaking louder and softer, higher and lower, and even pausing to create anticipation before the next event in the story unfolds. When a favorite book is well known to the child, the reader can playfully change a word and allow the child to correct their "silly" mistake. Sharing a laugh and having young children be "right" can add another dimension to the joy of reading. Even if sitting still is hard work, a reading time that is short, sweet, and relevant contributes to a love of reading.

Books become seeds of early conversations about the meaning of written text, a skill that the teacher calls "reading comprehension." Questions are powerful teaching

Your child is not the only one learning. *You* are learning to parent, and though it may seem that each developmental stage feels like returning to kindergarten, skills learned early on will come in handy later, too. For instance, when you patiently wait for your answer to the question, "Can you find the red ball?" you are practicing the important skill of *listening to your child.* This is enormously important at all ages, and especially so in the teen years. There is a not-so-distant future where you will want to know what your teen is really thinking and feeling. The trust and skills developed in their early childhood will pave the way for these successful interactions.

For many, the library can create an inexpensive outing to share as a family. If, however, you have difficulty managing younger siblings or finding a time that works around jobs and naps, most libraries have online search options that allow parents to pre-select and reserve books. This means that the time involved at the library for check-out/pick-up is nearly equal to the time it takes to go through a drive-through.

tools. At first the questions should be kept concrete and object-focused:

"Where is the chicken?"

"Can you find the red ball?"

"How many boys do you see?"

"What kind of animal is George?"

Later, they can become a part of the storyline:

"What do you think the stuck little truck will do next?"

"What do you think the puppy is feeling about his day right now?"

Parents can also model how they use books to learn more. If the heavy equipment machines your child sees through the car window fascinate her, you could take a trip together to the local library to find a picture book of big machines. Not only are they fun to look at, your child can learn the names and functions of these interesting contraptions.

WRITE TOGETHER

Learning to recognize letters, both upper- and lowercase and particularly those of their name, is another gift parents give their preschoolers that prepares them for reading. Children love to know the letters of "THEIR name." After learning these, they will naturally ask about the letters for "Mom" and "Dad," and the names of siblings and pets. Walks through the grocery store allow another chance to recognize "their letters" being used in other words and labels. Providing children with writing tools will invite an interest in learning to create those letters themselves. At this age, children should not be burdened with demands for clear letters, spacing, or staying on the line, but rather, letter creation should be playful, encouraged, and exciting. Also, larger crayons and markers can prevent small muscles from cramping, which could otherwise take the joy out of "writing their name" on a page they colored for Grandpa.

DON'T PANIC

Remember: Just as children understand what is said to them long before they can speak themselves, they will need to listen to many words and stories before they are ready to begin reading. By creating a positive relationship with words and conversation, books and letters, you have helped your child develop a strong foundation for reading comprehension. However, processing letters and sounds quickly as a novice reader will remain a huge challenge.

There are occasions when teachers of children in late kindergarten and first grade may express concern about the level of progress and suggest remedial help. If this is the case, first: do not panic. Reports from reading specialists suggest that with early and consistent support, children are able to overcome hurdles and become highly competent readers. So, do listen closely for suggestions of activities being taught at school that can be reinforced at home (remember to keep these fun and engaging). And do seek further assessments to help identify specific issues. Finally, work with the reading specialists in your school setting or find a provider who is able to engage and support your learner.

Children at this early stage of education will need emotional support as well as academic support when faced with reading challenges. It is difficult for anyone— even an adult—to maintain interest and motivation if the challenge feels too great for too long. Further, psychologists suggest

Some teachers and schools set a great deal of emphasis on extrinsic (external) motivation strategies, such as stickers and reward systems. These strategies often bring short-term interest to an individual or classroom. Intrinsic (internal) motivation based on joy and developing self-confidence will help sustain children through later academic challenges.

that intrinsic (internal) motivation is impacted by one's belief about one's basic ability ("I am smart"), one's worth ("I am good"), and one's expectations of success ("I can do it"). Parents are in a unique place in a child's life to recognize and intervene if it appears a child is shifting to a self-defeating mindset.

BE A MODEL READER

Eventually, there will be a shift in the school curriculum from learning to read to reading to learn. Until that time, we as parents must remain aware of our children's interest in talking, letters, words, stories, and books, and continue to support, encourage, and maintain positive interest in reading. We do this by being model readers ourselves. By pointing out how reading is helping (while shopping, reading the paper, or paying bills) or when having fun with reading (enjoying a magazine while waiting), we help children see reading as another exciting part of growing up.

To encourage further interest, consider the places you take your child shopping. Rather than always going to the toy aisle, a trip to the book or magazine sections can expand children's access to books and stories that interest them. When family members are considering gift ideas, suggest that they explore some of the high-quality magazines available for even the youngest of children. After all, it's exciting for children to get mail sent directly to them. Remember: reading is one of life's simple pleasures. By talking together, reading together, writing together, remaining calm in the face of any learning challenges and modeling good reading practices, you can help lay the foundation for your child's lifelong engagement with reading.

ROUTINES: WHY AND WHICH ONES?

For decades, parents have been told about the importance of routines for children, but until recently we've never understood their value from the perspective of brain development. We've known that the flow of a parent and child's day together is much easier when both of them know the "what" and "when" of the day. Infants who have regular schedules, such as being awakened at the same time each day in preparation for transfer to daycare, soon exhibit behaviors that signal their awareness of the daily pattern. Often these infants will begin to set their "internal clock" for rousing on their own. Toddlers who have regular routines that signal when it is time to leave or clean up may begin to express disappointment at the first signal that the activity is approaching an end. The "clean up" song at daycare may be cause for a few moments of tears until the next activity begins. So, it should come as no surprise that by the time children are preschoolers, routines are important for successful transitions in daily life.

Some of this importance has to do with the wonders of the brain. The brain has a certain capacity for working memory, through which we can be active participants in conversation, exploration, learning or responding to stimuli. As we mature, some of those early learning pieces become "chunks" of content that can be stored in long-term memory, which literally frees some brain space for the working memory. A task like putting on socks as a preschooler demands deep engagement of working memory to manage all the hand, eye, and foot coordination to be successful. As the repetition continues, the whole task becomes a well-coordinated process that takes less and less thought and active memory to complete. For many children, by the time they have entered kindergarten they recognize socks as only one small step in the whole process of getting dressed. The process of putting on socks has been stored in the long-term memory as a "chunk" that may still at times be frustrating because the fingers may not be strong enough for what the mind knows "should work."

Getting ready for preschool can be a major struggle for children. When we consider just how many separate tasks are needed in the process of getting ready

Since every brain has to deal with the limitations of working memory, it is important to guard children from too many other distractors during these high stress points of the day. A television show or favorite toy may hijack the brain by capturing the attention of the mind and eye and keeping a child from focusing on the required task.

to leave (eating, getting dressed, toileting), it is a wonder that any family manages to be on time for anything! Routines for any of the tasks will ease the larger process for everyone involved. Simple charts help to support a flow by helping children track where they are in the process. These charts can also be an aid for the parent who does not want to engage in constant verbal reminders of each step along the way.

If the family wants to have a celebration of the child's success at managing "getting ready," they can offer opportunities within regular family patterns for special acknowledgment. Something like being able to choose the family dinner or dessert at the end of the week or choosing the toppings on a pizza can often be enough to give children a sense of acknowledgment for their work. These celebrations acknowledge that learning self-care skills are important without becoming an added expense or disrupting a family budget to buy something extra.

	MON.	TUE.	WED.	THUR.	FRI.	SAT.
🩲	⭐					
👕	⭐					
👖	⭐					
👟						

Bedtimes become a parental nightmare when children have no well-developed routines or positive rituals for the transition to sleep. Preschool children who earlier had positive rituals and routines may begin to explore new patterns. (See *Sleep,* page 169.)

Parents sometimes want very much to be able to control when and how long children sleep. However, this is an area in which parents may set a context for positive sleep patterns, but external control of sleep is rarely possible. Sleep may be natural but it is not always easy. It can be impacted not only by individual biology, but also by social and environmental factors.

There are, however, some areas in which parents do have control.

The sleep environment. Is the room too full of distractors? Children and adults may self-sabotage by engaging in reading or other activity and miss the smoothest window for sleep transition. It is important for parents to be aware when the child may find the environment too stimulating to settle. When siblings share a sleep space they will have to learn how to settle.

Screen time. Recent research has found that exposure to electronic screens will disrupt the brain's circadian rhythm (wake-sleep cycle) by impacting the brain's ability to use light to signal the body when sleep should occur. There are aftermarket products that filter screen displays to minimize disruption, but overall the recommendation is to prohibit screen time two hours before a child is expected to sleep.

Diet. Children who are on growth spurts may waken especially early due to hunger. Even those who have eaten a well-balanced dinner may need additional food added to their bedtime routine for a period of time.

Overstimulation. Stimulation is an important part of growing and learning, but too much of a good thing is still too much! Because life is real, there will be occasions when company may stay too late, when children are rushed too much, or when play has been too intense immediately before bedtime. If, however, there is a pattern of too much and too fast, children are likely to become overtired. There is a myth that overtiring children will make them sleep better. Unfortunately, many overtired children find themselves unable to transition to sleep. Others rouse often during sleep and still others are unable to manage self-regulation, which results in disruptive behaviors during the day.

Nightmares and night terrors. Sleep is an important time for the brain to sort and store new learning. Our creative processes are uninhibited during dreaming, which means that as we process a day the images and thoughts may become jumbled and create a dream that is less than pleasant, resulting in a nightmare. Visual images and sounds that an adult finds innocuous may have more impact than expected on the mind of a child. Children traumatized by extreme life experiences may experience nightmares that need professional intervention to resolve, however, for most children, occasional nightmares are a normal part of growing up. Children who wake with a nightmare can be physically soothed and often return to sleep without continuing disruption. (See *Coping Strategies,* page 15.)

Children who experience night terrors often call out and have open eyes but are not awake and cannot be soothed or comforted. When they wake in the morning they give no indication of having had a bad dream or remembering any attempts to soothe them during the night, which makes night terrors far more troubling for parents than for the child. Because night terrors are associated with growth spurts in some children, they often occur several days in a row. They represent a disruption in the sleep cycle and usually occur at about the same time, so that parents may come to expect that if they are to occur it will be at or near the same time as the prior night. With this information, some parents have had success in partially rousing (NOT fully waking) the sleeping child about fifteen minutes before the expected event. This allows the child to reset their sleep cycle without coming to the point of full conscious arousal. Parents who have successfully transferred a sleeping child from car seat to crib have seen the process in which there is some small physical shuffle as the child resettles. Families who have a history of sleep talking or sleep walking know that the only real issue is keeping a non-awake person safe during the event.

Finally, parents are in charge of **setting the family's clock** to support the child's biological clock. In an ideal world, children should be able to wake rested on their own. When children are growing they need more sleep. Children who struggle to rise in the morning will need additional support. The strategy that is least disruptive to families is to move the bedtime earlier in fifteen-minute increments every two to three days until the child is getting enough sleep to transition to sleep and waken easily at the appropriate hour. To spare children from having to struggle to reset their wake-sleep cycles it is helpful to avoid extending bedtime significantly on weekends and holidays.

Families with children of every age develop patterns that define their days. Those that have positive routines for chores and challenging periods of the day like getting ready in the morning often have reduced levels of conflict and are freer to relax and enjoy their time with one another.

STRATEGIES FOR BUILDING ROUTINES THAT WORK FOR US!

- Check in with yourself. Are you carrying out routine tasks that could or possibly should be done by or with children?

- Analyze the task to identify specific roles for children and adults. For example, dinner requires not only meal preparation on the part of the adults, but also table setting, which can be managed by a preschooler (minus sharp utensils and pouring). Anything that requires heat or knives will have to be delayed until children are mature enough to be safe managing them.

- Share the activity! Yes, it is possible to learn to enjoy food preparation, laundry, and surface cleaning when it is shared.

- Remove obvious distractors such as TV, video games, etc.

- Add one new task/routine at a time rather than trying to create a whole new family culture in one attempt. For example, choose one area of life for attention—like the tasks of meal preparation. Once established, add new routines at other times of the day.

- Plan for 6-8 weeks for the new routine to be fully integrated.

There are so many benefits to children when they share chores with parents. The first is that when we work together we often have conversations. At the most basic level, conversations expand vocabulary. At another level, children learn patterns for managing time and tasks. Nutritionally, food resistance lessens when children are engaged in preparing meals. And, there is a boost to self-esteem in knowing that even the smallest person has value and contributes to the family.

GETTING OUT THE DOOR

It's funny that what we find so delightful in children can also be what we find most frustrating. For instance, a six-year-old's detailed examination of leaves on a fall walk can warm Mom's heart. That same six-year-old's detailed examination of the cereal box on Tuesday morning when she should have her shoes on and be out the door to school—that's a different kind of feeling in Mom's heart.

Why is it so hard to get children out the door?!

It's obvious, but well worth stating: One person (you!) must manage the coats, the hats, the lunches, the shoes, the everything of your own person, plus two, three, or even four more. In itself, the job is challenging, and added to this challenge are the facts that...

- The typical morning routine does not match a young child's physiological development. The young brain, in order to grow and learn, must be open and absorbent. Developmentally, it is very hard to be "on task."

- The morning routine is not only developmentally hard, but the child is often asked to do it without any motivation. Your child loves you, but hurrying her so that you are not late to work is not the fuel that is going to drive her engine. She needs a reason to want to get out the door—a motivation that is separate from your own need to not get fired!

These may sound like big hurdles to a more peaceful morning, but they are not insurmountable hurdles. Understanding your child's developmental abilities and considering what the morning routine looks like (and feels like) from your child's perspective will help you rethink this daily struggle.

Also, when you remember that your child's dilly-dallying is not personal; that it is not an intentional act meant to make you late; that it is not, in itself, a sign of ADD; and that it is a sign that your child is a kid, then it is easier to let go of the built-up frustrations and to make some changes that will help everyone get out the door with less struggle and stress.

IDEAS TO HELP EASE THE MORNING ROUTINE

Generally applies to all ages

The Night Before

(Yes, the morning routine actually begins the day before.)

Pack lunches as everyone is leaving the dinner table. (You're handling food anyway!)

- It may be helpful to keep the grocery list nearby to note items as they're getting low.

Set out next-day clothes at bedtime.

- For young children, have two appropriate options they can choose from (the child can practice limited choice and feel a sense of control).

- Older preschool children can pick out clothes and pack backpacks, thinking ahead to the next day's activities. (If needed, prompt the child to think about what the season may demand—sweaters, long pants.)

Make the "next-day agenda" part of the goodnight ritual.

- Verbally rehearse the next morning: "Tomorrow is preschool day. After breakfast Daddy will take you. You'll see Mrs. K and Mike and Suzie…"

- Be sure to close your ritual with a message of love.

Get children to bed early enough that they can be fully rested to begin the day.

- If you know your child is slow to transition from sleep to wake, also allow time for your child to "wind up."

- If needed, allow extra time for toilet learning or dressing skills.

The Morning

(Note: sometimes we are so hurried the love message gets lost—make sure there are treasured moments in your morning routine, be it a morning snuggle, goodbye ritual, etc.)

1. Follow the airplane metaphor: "Secure your oxygen mask first before assisting others."

    • Get up early enough to get yourself together before the rush of other's needs begins (this may mean that you are dressed and then covered with a robe or over-shirt to stay clean).

    • Be sure *you* are completely ready to go out the door before you gather children or say, "Let's go." All the work that went into getting the child to the door may be lost if you must move off somewhere to look for your keys.

2. Routine, routine, routine.

    Once established, routines prime the child for what is coming next, easing how much you must push and remind. Routines and rituals also plant the seeds of autopilot and help build trust that their world makes sense and is manageable.

    A sample routine may be:

    • Wake + five-minute snuggle

    • Dress

    • Breakfast

    • Teeth and face

    • Goodbye ritual (A family hug, a kiss of blessing for each child and adult on their way—this is yours to create for your family.)

3. Chart/Timer

    • Some children enjoy checking off tasks; some may enjoy a game of "beat the clock."

4. Avoid the media roadblocks! TV may sidetrack young minds.

- Visual images make it harder for the child to focus on the tasks of eating and dressing.

- Plus, TV shows have their own schedule, and once you turn it on you are adding the opportunity for pushback—"But the show's not over yet!"—into the mix.

5. Be aware of background noise.

- Radios playing in the background may pull adult attention and/or add to stress at the beginning of the day.

The Distraction

You cannot expect a young child to value what you value—getting to work on time, having a good breakfast to start the day, etc. You need to find something that the child values. For the younger child, this will likely be something tangible and fun—like permission to use the key fob to open the car door, or first one ready gets to choose the music on the way to daycare. For the kindergarten child, it might be experiencing natural consequences like being too late for playground time before the school day begins.

HOW TO HELP YOUR CHILD GET BACK ON TRACK

The young child will need almost constant attention to perform almost any task, but when she gets distracted you can:

- Refocus with a question (questions get attention better than statements).

  "You know what? This is the time that we eat our cereal."

- Make it fun.

  "Can you catch those Os on your spoon?"

- Remind the child of something she values.

  This is typically something immediate that you have built into the morning routine, perhaps a shoes-on song, a hold-hands walk to the car or bus stop, or, to borrow a potty training idea, a sticker for every successful morning.

For the kindergarten+ child, the tools are still useful, but now the child can also be reminded of and motivated by natural consequences.

- Remind him of a positive consequence he values (some examples below):

  "Remember, if we finish in time I can walk in with you…"

  "Remember, at school your friends are waiting to see you…"

  "You sure are growing up. You know exactly what we need to do to get to school on time." (Remember the value that motivates the child may simply be his own feeling of competence.)

Of course…some mornings will be crazy and breakfast will be a bag of cereal in the car or shoes will go on the feet in the backseat. It's not a big deal (if it's occasional!).

TRANSITIONS

Every day is filled with transitions: wake up, clothes on, mealtime, shoes on, in the car, out of the car, preschool (which has its own list of transitions), lunch, naptime, big sister home, dinner, playtime, clean-up time, bath, stories and prayers, into bed, sleep.

Young children live in the moment. When they are engaged in an activity, they are developmentally unable to split attention from their immediate focus. Transitions, by their nature, are often perceived as interruptions. Preparation—telling the child about the change before it happens and as it happens—can ease the stress of transitions. Tools that signal change and offer a new focus can help the child shift from one activity to the next, while rituals and routines provide anchors in a day filled with constant stimuli and little control.

The preschool brain is developing Executive Function—the complex set of mental processes that enables us to plan and organize, to anticipate and adapt, to focus and order, and to understand time and its passing. The oft repeated tasks—eating, putting on socks—will move from a series of small steps demanding total absorption into a coordinated set of tasks (time sequenced, organized) that become part of one's "autopilot." Because his brain is still developing, he needs you, for now, to be his Executive Function to help buffer the bumps of his day.

The preschool child's developmental drive is to become more competent through doing. Speech is a wonderful new tool, but the world is still experienced with her whole body. Tasks that require stillness—the car seat, the dinner table, sleep—are biologically hard and may invite active resistance. She may need encouragement, support, empathy, and help to accomplish tasks that are off-step with her internal drive.

Transitions:

Use these steps to help your preschooler make the transition from one activity to the next

THE STORY OF GETTING OUT THE DOOR:

Chapter 1
We will eat our cereal.
We will put on our shoes.
We will put on our coat.
We will get in the car and
We will go to the store.

Chapter 2
Cereal all done.
Now we put on shoes.
This one first or the other one first?

Chapter 3
Shoes on! Yay! Now we find our coats. Can you find your coat?
I will find my coat, too.

Chapter 4
We are ready to get in the car and go to the store, where you can sit in the cart and help Daddy shop...

Give the child a sense of control by offering two acceptable choices.

Model the task for the child by working in parallel.

FIRST

TELL THE STORY of what will come next.

Allow TIME for the child to take each step.

UPDATE the story as steps are accomplished.

IF

the child is UPSET or RESISTING a transition, show empathy.

You wish we could stay. You are sad!

SHOW EMPATHY & GIVE WORDS TO FEELINGS
Give words to the emotion the child is experiencing. Mirror the emotion in your facial expression and body language. The child needs to know you understand that she is upset. Until she does, she is likely to continue to "tell" you.

THEN to support and ease the transition use any or all of these additional transition tools [🔵T]:

A child has enough fears. Do not add to them by threatening to leave the child behind.

> When we visit the zoo again we will see the gorillas and the lion... maybe the lion will ROAR!...and we will...

> At home you can play with your toy lion and tell Dad about the zoo. What will you tell him about first?

USE IMAGINATION
Offer the child in imagination what he cannot have at that moment. Be specific. It may help to add a silly or unexpected element—*Maybe the lion will be having a tea party...*

LOOK FORWARD
Show the child the future. Be positive about what is next.

MAKE IT A GAME
Skip. Tip-toe. Walk like an animal. Race. Games make hard work fun and can also become helpful rituals.

> You pick up the blue blocks, I'll pick up the red ones

> Let's sing our clean-up song:
> *We have had a busy day*
> *Time to put our toys away*
> *When we get the job all done*
> *We'll sing and read and have more fun.*

SING A SONG
Specific songs for specific tasks are not only fun, but provide cues to the steps needed to accomplish the task.

BRRRING!

> "Aww! The timer says it's time to go."

> "Remember, when you get in your car seat that's when you have your special snack!"

OBJECT
Bring one along. If it is safe and legal, take one (such as a leaf from the playground). Objects can offer security.

TIMER/CLOCK
Let a timer announce when to leave or to stop. Be your child's partner— you are as disappointed as she is.

ACKNOWLEDGMENT
A special snack, a special book or activity acknowledges the hard work the child is doing.

Remember: Transitions are hard but they do get easier as they are practiced.

TRANSITIONS: USE THESE STEPS TO HELP YOUR CHILD MAKE THE TRANSITION FROM ONE ACTIVITY TO THE NEXT

What if nothing's working?

With a strong, steady body, calm muscles and firm follow-through, you will have to step in, explaining matter-of-factly as you go: *I'll put your coat in the car. You can put it on before we go into preschool. Remember, to play outside today, you'll need your coat.* The child, in all likelihood, will be upset. Continue to use Empathy and Naming Feelings and, if you feel the child will respond, try some transition tools again. (Some children will be better able to self-calm if the adult no longer offers words or additional input.)

Is my child's need for a transitional object (blanket, stuffed toy) a sign of weakness?

No. A child's attachment to the object is often a portable reminder of the love and attachment of his caregivers. This is a human trait. Immigrant stories often include a mention of particular objects that were emotional reminders of "love and home."

Isn't what you call "acknowledgment" just a bribe?

Rewards are part of life, even for adults. We all find ways to help ourselves complete tasks that are particularly difficult. You can sidestep the language of bribery by avoiding *if-then* statements in favor of *when-then* statements. "*Remember, when you're all dry after bath, that's when you pick out the stories for you and Daddy to read.*"

Are transition tools just distractions?

At times, yes. But transition tools are doing more. Songs encourage language, articulation, and listening skills. Empathy and Naming Feelings help develop emotional intelligence. Routines plant the seeds for autopilot. Rituals carry a sense of family warmth into future memories.

Transitions are not only changes the child engages in, but changes to the environment, such as the reentry of a parent who has been working outside the home or a sibling who has been at school.

Transitions that involve separation from loved ones are often the most challenging. (For more discussion of *Separation*, see page 159.)

SETTING THE GROUNDWORK FOR SMOOTHER TRANSITIONS

1. Ask yourself if your expectations are realistic. Is the day too hurried? Is the child asked to get in the car seat too often or expected to sit still too long? See if you can adjust your expectations, while keeping your values intact. For instance, if you value both a rested child and the need for him to spend time with late-working Mom, then record Mom's voice reading his favorite stories so that he can have her presence as part of his bedtime ritual.

2. Create patterns around things that you do every day. Start with those things that occur around the same time each day. Examples include a small-person chore before mealtime (carry spoons to the table) or a nightly piggy-back ride to bed. Rituals and routines provide anchors in a huge, fast-moving world.

3. Create opportunities for the child to experience control and competency. For instance, offer two choices, both of which you can live with ("Jacket or sweater today?" "Jammies first or brush teeth?"); work in parallel ("Mama's getting her shoes on, too." "You're picking up trucks, I'm picking up books."); act inept to let the child show off his abilities ("Socks go on ears, right? I can't find the seat belt straps. I wonder who can show me…").

4. Make it visual. Have a calendar or chart with pictures representing what

will happen that day. For example, the child can mark off each before-bed task as it is accomplished. When reviewing her picture calendar, a child can help pack her school bag to be ready for preschool tomorrow.

5. When possible, be flexible. If the child is MEGA-resistant, let natural consequences communicate the rule: *The safety rule for the playground says you must wear shoes. We can go play when you get your shoes on. We can watch until you're ready.*

6. Carry an easily accessible timer with you. Allow the timer to "tell" the child when the transition will occur. Give verbal preparation for when the timer will cue everyone. For instance: *The timer says we have three minutes before it's time to go. That's enough time for you to go down the slide two more times.*

7. Use the child's special number to support transition. *People who are four get to spend four more minutes in the backyard. Then it's time to go in and clean up.*

SEPARATION

Did you ever think about how hard it is to leave someone you love? Even as an adult this can be tough. Yet, separations are a part of life. For children, separation tasks are an important part of cognitive, social, and emotional development. Because these tasks involve interplay between internal growth and environment (nature and nurture), there are things adults can do to help as children grow through the challenges of separation.

WHAT ARE "SEPARATION" TASKS?

One separation task is the work of being able to handle being apart from Mom and Dad. When a child fusses as you leave, or wants you to continually share every part of her play, she is focused on learning to be away from you.

To support the challenges of this task:

- Start small. Use as many short everyday leavings as possible for your child to practice. These may be as simple as the time you take to load clothes in a washer or get the mail. Report to your child that you are leaving and reassure her that you will return quickly. If the child is anxious, remind him of things he can do while he waits for you and offer brief words of celebration when he manages the time without you.

- Become comfortable with your child's concrete reminders of you: security blankets, etc.

- Set up a play area near you where your child can see or easily hear you, but which allows you to be slightly removed from his immediate space. It is OK to maintain the feeling of companionship by being part of the conversation about the play, but still not actually engage in the play. This creates opportunity to practice some independence.

- Although it may be tempting, do not sneak away when the child is not aware. It is one thing to create some distance, another to disappear. Any perceived benefit of avoiding an emotional response from the child in the moment is offset by the creation of greater issues of anxiety for children who worry that their parents may disappear with no notice.

- Think about space. There can be places in a home that just feel "too far away." Having a play space in a basement or a room that is set apart might look like good space management on paper, but when children are fearful they will rarely use a separate space without their most trusted adult with them.

A second separation task is the work of being able to handle being with people who are new. When children are generally content to spend some time playing on their own (with regular check-ins with their primary adult, of course), but suddenly stick like glue when guests come to visit, it is likely that they are focused on learning to handle being with people who are new.

To support this task:

- Whenever possible, allow time for the entry process. It may be that the adults engage in some greetings before offering the opportunity to interact with the child.

- Avoid labels such as "shy."

- Do intervene when an adult is overzealous in his or her approach to your child. Reassure both the adult and the child that there is no hurry.

- For children who need a few extra moments of time to warm up, allow the child to determine when she is ready for interaction with an adult. A delay in responding to new people may be perceived by some as rudeness. Remember that preschool children are still learning the patterns/manners of greeting. It is important for young learners to be challenged but not overwhelmed by stress when practicing new skills. For older children who know the manners of greeting but are still challenged, the following suggestions may be a better fit.

- Role-playing general greetings, like how to say hello to a guest, can be practiced at times when guests are not present. Using children's favorite toys as props, parents can create play opportunities that incorporate more practice in greeting and exiting skills.

- When possible, spend a few moments prior to guests arriving to prepare your child for their entry. Coaching can be as simple as: "Remember that you can give them the gift of a hello when they come in the door."

If children in very familiar settings such as their own home develop increased anxiety greeting others or become increasingly unable to relax in the presence of new people, it may be time to seek professional guidance before children begin to build a pattern of social withdrawal.

When the situation demands both tasks at once, such as staying with a babysitter, entering the first day of school, or an overnight at a friend's house, the work can be more than twice as hard!

- Telling ahead of time what to expect is helpful for some children. Again, watch your child, as too much telling can create additional anxiety in some children.

- Explore the new environment when there is no expectation of being left there. Learning about the classroom may provide an anchor to buffer the addition of new adults and children.

- Leave a token of yourself with the child, saying something like, "Will you take care of this for me while I'm gone?" The object can be tucked in a school bag or pocket to provide a solid link to you in your absence.

- Be very specific about when the child will be picked up and by whom. For example, "Dad will pick you up today after school. He will come to the classroom to find you."

After an initial period of adjustment in which the environment, routines, and people become familiar, children learn to separate with budding confidence in themselves, as well as trust in your return. This does not mean that once learned there is never another twinge when new milestones involve separation. For adults, college, a new job, or a new city carry echoes of our early separations. At these times, we rely on our more mature skills and more fully developed confidence from the seeds planted in this early stage of our development.

TURNING LOOSE— INDEPENDENT PLAYDATES

As children enter social environments where they have access to a larger number of potential friends, sooner or later they want more time to play than school can provide. No longer is the child's social network entirely under the control of the parent, who can determine which children and adults will be a part of the child's life experience.

Inviting a friend over to play is a milestone not only for the child, but also for the parents involved. It may be the first time that a child is invited into a home in which the parent does not know the other child or the other parent! With some prior planning, this can be a great opportunity to expand friendships for both children and adults.

Often in families it will fall to one of the adults to function as the social secretary—coordinating personal calendars, setting and maintaining the schedule of outside events. There are key questions that need to be addressed when adding a child's social calendar to that of the family. Answering the following questions provides a safety net for children through their adolescence.

Who? Answering the question is more than finding out the names of the children who are interested in playing with yours. When supporting young children with independent playdates it means knowing the "who" and also the "who else." For safety, before dropping a child off for a playdate, it is helpful to know not only the other parent, but who else will have access to the children while they play. Are there older siblings, relatives, or family friends around? How will they relate to the children? One way to answer these kinds of questions is to take gradual steps in supporting the independent visit, by planning for some parent-to-parent or whole family get-togethers. At first, these can be relatively uncomplicated events like meeting at a playground or inviting the family for a simple meal and visiting with the adults while the children play.

Where? To avoid creating more stress than necessary, consider playdates that involve outdoor play. When inclement weather makes this difficult, families may find it helpful to take turns hosting AND add a clean-up ritual at the end of the playtime so that the hosting family will not be faced with an additional burden of picking up after guests have gone home. The answer to where a playdate occurs may involve decisions about a variety of other socially difficult circumstances, for example, allowing a child to play in a home where there are guns, where TV or video games are used to entertain, or profanity is common.

How long? This too is an important question involving more than just when to pick up the child. For families with younger siblings, long playdates may disrupt nap schedules. Too-long playdates may have children struggling to enjoy their time together. Even peers of the same age may have different levels of physical and emotional stamina, so that what would be a wonderful experience is ruined by being a half an hour too long. Children who pair often will develop natural rhythms to their play. For example, time in an imaginary fort may last for twenty to forty minutes before a renegotiation of the activity. These naturally occurring shifts may be the time for Mom to check in and encourage a pause for a water break or light snack.

What? Often preschool children will have begun to internalize "house rules" for boundaries of play that allow them to use their imaginations and energy spending time with their friend in safe and enjoyable ways. However, even teenagers have trouble at times with guiding a peer. Parents hosting child guests may be called upon to suggest alternatives or to limit certain activities to ensure the safety of siblings, pets, and household items. At other times, parents may want to limit activities like video games based on family household rules/values.

OTHER CONSIDERATIONS FOR INDEPENDENT PLAYDATES

A difficult friend

Sometimes children will express special interest in spending time with peers that the parents find difficult. Parental discomfort can result for several reasons—the intensity of play the children engage in with one another; the guest child's inexperience or inability to relate to younger siblings in the hosting family; or the less-than-desirable behavior that the guest child seems to bring out in the host family's child.

Intensity is often managed by arranging playdates that allow big/gross muscle play. Music and stop-and-go games may help a parent manage any sense of over-whelm related to how big and how loud some preschool play can be.

For guests inexperienced with younger siblings, host parents may find they have to coach preschoolers (see *Coaching* or *Shadowing*, page 46) to ensure the safety of younger siblings. Since younger siblings are very likely to want to share in the novelty of an older friend, parents may also have to direct younger siblings into satisfying play separate from the older children so that big sisters and brothers can enjoy having a classmate visit.

Parents may be embarrassed by seeing their child's behavior choices in the presence of a peer

Addressing children in the moment will help coach children to understand the behavior expected in your home. For example, *"Oops, it looks like you're forgetting how we do it at our house. Help your friend know the way we do it here."* Other examples include strategies that *report what you see*, such as, *"Sophie, it looks like you were thinking it's OK to push your little sister away when Angie is visiting. Even when we have company we keep each other safe. If you need help, let me know."* Or, strategies that *assert your adult leadership*, such as, *"You know what, Henry? At our house, children do not play in the bathroom. You and George need to play in the living room."*

Building confidence

Independent playdates are an opportunity to gain self-confidence and anchor friendships for children who may be hesitant in large groups. When hosting a friend, the child can practice basic leadership skills of assertion and collaboration in the known and safe environment of home. If a child appears dominated in his or her own turf when certain friends are over, practicing with younger children or other friends can be equally helpful.

FOOD AND FAMILY

In parenting circles, there is more and more discussion about the importance of the shared family meal. Many experts and doctors support the idea, and the research seems to back it up. But some of these benefits of eating together are more obvious than others. For instance, food and conversation go together, thus the notion that family dinnertime helps language development in young children is not a hard sell. But the research is also telling us that the family meal is a strong protector against risky adolescent behaviors, including drug and alcohol use. But what is it about family mealtime that could possibly influence such behavior? No study yet points to a definitive cause, but it's likely the answer has something to do with a mix of the following:

- The family meal is likely to be nutritionally sound and nutrition affects development and behavior.

- Family mealtime is a ritual. Rituals can ground individuals and increase a sense of security. Where the expected is consistently realized, there is fertile ground for trust.

- Shared meals support attachment. We know best those with whom we share meals.

So, the message is that eating together is important. YET, take this theory off the page and into the dining room of a family with young children who won't eat, or won't sit still, or who get "creative" with food, and a parent can begin to wonder how it is that family mealtime can be so beneficial. If you are a parent who finds dinner with children stressful and even unpleasant, there is no need to feel worried for your future teenager, or to feel criticized. Food battles are extremely common in families with young children. The good news is there are many ways to ease the stress that will also lay the groundwork in your family for a continued positive relationship with food and with one another.

TAKING THE PRESSURE OFF MEALTIME

The basic formula sounds easy: The parent is responsible for providing nutritionally sound food. The child is responsible for eating (and choosing how much). The end.

Yet, anyone who has nurtured a child from infancy knows that food is deeply connected to love. The focus on adequate nutrition for newborns is intense, and for a parent to step back from that intensity is by no means easy. There was a time in the not-too-distant past when the adult was once solely responsible for feeding the child. Now, that child is becoming responsible for feeding himself. That is a huge transition (for the adult!). As parents, we push or withhold food because we want our children to have the best nutrition, yet too much pushing and withholding can inadvertently lead to a relationship with food that is less about nutrition and more about struggle, power, control, and sometimes, solace. To help take you out of the food battle, keep these six points in mind:

- Research shows that, when left to make their own choices, **children will, over time, eat in a way that is nutritionally balanced.**

- **Each meal does not have to be nutritionally "perfect."** It is what is eaten over the course of a day—some pediatricians suggest over the course of a week—that matters. So, if on Tuesday your child is on a cereal kick, it can be balanced with protein and other essential nutrients on Wednesday or Thursday.

- **Understanding portion size** can help you resist the urge to "push" food and invite power struggles. In general, a serving size is one measured tablespoon per year for a young child. How many chunks of green bean can fit in a measured tablespoon—two or three? When a preschool-age child has eaten four bites of green beans, she has probably eaten an amount appropriate to her age and size. If four ounces (an adult portion) of meat protein is the size of a deck of playing cards, a child who has eaten two to three bites has, again, probably eaten an amount appropriate for his age and size.

- **Understand that your child may have his own internal eating clock.** He may love a big breakfast and prefer lighter fare for dinner. Or he may not be ready for much food until mid-morning. Noticing and planning your offerings to match your child's preferences can create a more positive relationship with food.

- **Expect fluctuations.** You may find that when your child is in a growth spurt, everything about serving size and interest in food will shift. Some days it may seem your child packs away more food than you! In the absence of power struggles over food, trust her body to eat what it needs to maintain the energy she needs.

- **Be aware of alternative sources of nutrition**. For instance, for the child not interested in meat, try beans or cubes of tofu for protein. You can find other alternatives for nutrients by using the USDA.gov website.

SHIFTING THE PATTERN

While keeping the above in mind can help you make good decisions about how to engage your child with food, if a push-resist pattern is already in place, or if food has been a successful way to engage Mom and Dad in the past, what else can you do to shift the pattern?

Turn the battleground into a playground

Invite your child to have fun with food. This can mean dressing food up—putting raisin eyes on pear halves or cutting food into shapes—and it can mean games—go ahead and have the broccoli-helicopter fly into the mouth. Providing a context for story may also give the child some control and fun in eating: *"That pea looks brave and adventurous. I think it wants to be the first to explore the cave."* The possibilities are endless.

Make a food chart

There is something about charts and children. Children love the "I did it!" feeling, and charts can make an accomplishment tangible and visual. Plus, there are all those fun stickers and smiley faces. An "I'm Trying New Foods" chart can help motivate a child to taste new things. Make the goal easy: Try one new food a week—just a taste—and you may find the child wants to try more. If you and your child shop together, you may enjoy talking about the food you see. Your child may take the lead and encourage you to try some with him.

Engage your child in the process of making food

Children are more likely to try what they have helped to make, plus, they get the added good feeling of being capable and helpful. Some of the world's most renowned chefs have fond memories of being invited, at a young age, into the kitchen to explore and contribute.

Though relaxed, lingering family dinners full of sparkling conversation may be quite a few years off, you are laying the groundwork for a healthy relationship to food and with each other. This will come in handy when busy schedules and after-school events present a new challenge to your family mealtime. An occasional hurried or missed family meal is to be expected, but the gift of maintaining a shared family table lasts a lifetime.

SLEEP

Although every child is different, there are average sleep requirements for children. Most preschool children need between ten and thirteen hours of sleep in a twenty-four-hour period. Over the elementary years, sleep requirements may begin to lessen somewhat, only to lengthen again as children experience growth spurts and the social and emotional demands of pre-adolescence.

Generally, three-year-old children will still need a nap or regular resting time each day. Most often, naps/resting periods are best begun between 12:30–1:30 p.m., which allows for lunch and a brief time of mini-ritual transition—perhaps a story— and may last one to two hours. For children near the age of four, the need for a nap may diminish. Parents are often familiar with the experience of children dropping a nap from earlier developmental stages when infants or toddlers went from three to two naps or from two naps to one.

Most active children need a rest period each day; for some, until the age of six. The rest period may entail some quiet activity such as reading a book, listening to music, or some minimally demanding physical activity such as snap-together blocks or puzzles. This quiet time allows for the possibility of sleep but does not demand that the child nap.

> There are children who give up daytime naps very early. Creating a regular time for rest and quiet activity in a safe space will allow the child to sleep when needed or practice independent play.

Lack of sleep for children may result in noticeable moodiness or irritability (as it does with adults). In addition to these emotional cues, a person who needs more sleep may express a variety of cognitive and self-regulation difficulties. For example:

- Inability to make any decision.
  - It's now too hard to choose which pjs to put on or which book to read.

- o This may also be noted by the inability to make good choices about getting along with others.

- Outbursts (crying, physical aggression, or verbal aggression) that seem unnecessary or have no apparent cause. This is especially true if it is near a resting time or going to sleep at night.

- Need for physical closeness to a parent or a special transition object (stuffed animal, pacifier, blanket, etc.).

- Excessive activity.

  - o For some high-active children, the more tired they become the more wound-up they become. Children who get a high-energy "second wind" may have missed the window of time in which they could have more easily transitioned to sleep.

HOW TO HELP

What parents can do to help establish a new sleeping pattern for preschool children so that they can get enough rest:

- Talk about what sleep does for our bodies. (*When we sleep, our bodies are able to grow big and strong. When we don't sleep enough, people get cranky and our bodies don't work right.*)

- Talk about everyone the child knows and that they sleep too (and perhaps talk about where they sleep).

- Decide, with the help and input of your child, on a nighttime ritual. Because every family and child is different, what works for one family or child may not be the best for another. Many families pick several different ideas to be part of the ritual. Here are some suggestions:

  - o Take a bath.

  - o Put pajamas on (an external cue to the child).

  - o Talk about the best part of the day while lying in bed.

  - o Read a book (about 15–30 minutes).

- ○ Turn on soothing music (maybe a lullaby CD from when s/he was a baby, ocean noises, whale songs, chants, "white" noise—like a fan).

- ○ Say prayers.

- ○ Sing a song or two (the same ones each night are best unless the child picks a different song).

- ○ Dim lights.

- ○ Lie down with your child or sit beside the bed with her for a few minutes (this can invite co-sleeping for very tired parents!).

- ○ Have a small quiet signal of when the parent will leave (at the end of the song or when a gentle timer goes off).

PITFALLS

One of the major pitfalls that may occur is when a child keeps asking for "one more" thing (another story, song, minute, glass of water, etc.). Parents must realize that by giving in to the child's request, they have just rewarded the behavior, and the child will expect the same treatment the next time.

Although it is REALLY hard for parents, the best thing that can be done for both child and parent is to say, "You want another story. Is that right?" PAUSE. "I understand that reading is a lot of fun. How many stories do we get to read at bedtime?" PAUSE FOR ANSWER AND THEN SAY EITHER, "That's right. How many stories have we read?" PAUSE, OR, "The rule is that we read __ stories at bedtime. Which story would you like for me to read after breakfast?" PAUSE. "You help remind me when you wake up in the morning which story you want to read. Goodnight."

Although the above scenario might not EXACTLY fit your situation, the keys are:

- To acknowledge your child's wants and feelings.

- Remind her what the rule is. (This is best if the child will say what the rule/routine is.)

- Plan a future time when "it" can happen (and follow through!) and ask for the child's help in this.

- DO NOT give in or the "one more thing" becomes part of the ritual.

The newest culprit contributing to children being unable to transition to sleep is too much exposure to the lighting of computers, tablets, and phone screens. The light waves from these tools (called blue light, but not perceived as blue when looking at them) disrupt the brain's ability to transition to sleep. It is recommended that access to these screens end two hours before bedtime.

Ideally, the time for sleep rituals should not be hurried. This challenges parents to consider how siblings share in end-of-day rituals. Remember that "turn taking" is an important part of a preschooler's understanding of the world. In a class, he has learned when it's his turn to be line leader. This practice is helpful in managing the emotions of "not right now." At first it may be disappointing that baby's night snack comes first, or that it is Daddy's turn to read the stories, but when parents stay calm, children do learn to trust that this is the way the world works in their family.

WILL IT WORK?

Although it takes time, it will work. Will this be easy? Not at first. The longer a child goes without an external routine to help in setting a body clock for wake and sleep, the harder it is to start one. After about two to three weeks, both child and parent will become more accustomed to "the rules" and things will begin to flow more easily. Remember that children are always growing and changing. This means that children will occasionally test the boundaries, and in some cases, adjustments in the routine will have to be made based on the child's new stage of development. In addition, sleep disturbances may occur when children are going through a cognitive growth spurt, are coming down with an illness, or have disruption in other parts of their day. Once well-developed sleep patterns are in place, when brief disruptions occur, children will quickly return to the "normal" that has been established.

PULLING IT TOGETHER AND MOVING FORWARD

Although focused on the preschool years, this book has introduced parenting skills that will continue to be relevant throughout the elementary and teen years. It will never cease to be important to honor the temperament of both parent and child, to recognize and respect the emotions that inform us when a boundary has been crossed, and to bring careful consideration to the context of problems before taking next steps.

Additional age- or topic-specific resources will continue to be helpful in keeping parenting skills sharp. Adults who care for children and families will always be kept on a growing edge. Remember that we learn in stages too. The stages look something like this:

Awareness. Sometimes we may consciously set a goal or seek a specific solution. At other times we become aware of our growing edge when we feel guilt or regret for some pattern we see in ourselves. Awareness is an important place to be if new patterns are to be learned. However, at this phase, we may be at risk of focusing so much on failure that we may overlook successes and fail to envision a positive future. Support from others is a good defense against discouragement. It is vital to resist the mindset "I'll never be able to do this," which is an invitation to stop growing as a parent.

Consciously competent. In this stage of learning people often report, "I can do it if I think about it." Learners have new content and are actively attempting to implement change. There's awareness of the old behavior and related outcomes, yet also a conscious attempt to use different words or behaviors. It can feel awkward or formulaic to be living through this learning stage, and some experience the sense of "it's not the real me" or somehow being phony. Actually, this is very much a "real me" as a "real" learner.

Unconsciously competent. At this stage, a skill has been practiced enough to become fully integrated or automatic. With a new autopilot, the mind is free to be more creative. Although you may still use phrases or patterns very much like *the book* *or teacher* suggested, you are now able to bring your own words, humor, and mental flexibility to problem-solving.

WHAT IS THE GOAL?

The goal is to be a parent with leadership patterns that continue to support children's growth and development. In other words, you are laying the foundation for your children to become fully competent people in their own right. We hope to raise children who are not only able to feed and dress themselves and manage the flow of their days, but who also come to more awareness of personal choices and their responsibility for the outcomes of those choices.

Much of that work is still before you. Infants nudge us to sophisticated problem-solving when we're sleep deprived. Toddlers nudge us to explore boundaries and establish shared discipline. Preschoolers nudge us to understand our individual and partnered responses to emotions. Elementary children nudge us to articulate our values, and our teens nudge us to deepen our understanding of independence and interdependence.

Remember that no matter how grown up *we* are, *they* will keep us growing if we can pay attention to ourselves too. Having read this book and continuing to explore these basic skills and expand your developmental knowledge, you are laying a solid foundation for those profound growth steps to come. You and your family are on an amazing journey. My best wishes are with you always.

ACKNOWLEDGMENTS

Any good parenting book is more than the words of the author. It can be thought of as a gemstone with facets that reflect thoughts, values, experience, and emotional support, as well as the nitty-gritty skills of graphic design, editing, and publishing. It is impossible to thank everyone. I would, however, like to express my gratitude to the focus group participants and members of the Mothers of Twins Club who helped narrow the child issues and clarify that when living with preschool children we need to be as attentive to ourselves and the other adults involved as we are to the children.

I also need to give a special note of thanks to Deanna Davis Hall for her contribution to the section on preschool sleep, as well as a statement of appreciation for the seminal work in parent and teacher education (1970s) of Jean Illsley Clarke, William Wayson, Gay Pinnell, Judith and Donald Smith.

Special thanks to Joshua Dedinsky, Ann Dennis, Amber Liston, Jennifer George, Sarah McCaig and Caren Keating Wildman for their thoughtful comments, Kendra Hovey and her husband Greg Bonnell for their vision of a graphic parenting book, and the team at Columbus Publishing Lab who brought the details together.

www.ingramcontent.com/pod-product-compliance
Lightning Source LLC
LaVergne TN
LVHW010314070426
835509LV00023B/3466